THE COMMON CORE STATE STANDARDS IN LITERACY SERIES

A series designed to help educators successfully
implement CCSS literacy standards in K–12 classrooms

SUSAN B. NEUMAN AND D. RAY REUTZEL, EDITORS

SERIES BOARD: Diane August, Linda Gambrell, Steve Graham, Laura Justice,
Margaret McKeown, and Timothy Shanahan

Reading Across Multiple Texts in the Common Core Classroom, K–5

JANICE A. DOLE, BRADY E. DONALDSON, AND REBECCA S. DONALDSON

Reading, Thinking, and Writing About History

Teaching Argument Writing to Diverse Learners in the Common Core Classroom, Grades 6–12

CHAUNCEY MONTE-SANO, SUSAN DE LA PAZ, AND MARK FELTON

Engaging Students in Disciplinary Literacy, K–6

Reading, Writing, and Teaching Tools for the Classroom

CYNTHIA H. BROCK, VIRGINIA J. GOATLEY, TAFFY E. RAPHAEL,
ELISABETH TROST-SHAHATA, AND CATHERINE M. WEBER

All About Words

Increasing Vocabulary in the Common Core Classroom, PreK–2

SUSAN B. NEUMAN AND TANYA WRIGHT

Reading

Across Multiple Texts

in the Common Core Classroom

K–5

Janice A. Dole

Brady E. Donaldson

Rebecca S. Donaldson

Foreword by Robert J. Marzano

TEACHERS
COLLEGE
PRESS

Teachers College, Columbia University
New York and London

Published by Teachers College Press, 1234 Amsterdam Avenue, New York, NY 10027

Library of Congress Cataloging-in-Publication Data

Dole, Janice A.
  Reading multiple texts in the common core classroom, K-5 / Janice A. Dole, Brady E. Donald-son, Rebecca S. Donaldson.
     pages cm
  Includes bibliographical references and index.
  ISBN 978-0-8077-5590-7 (pbk. : alk. paper)
  ISBN 978-0-8077-7333-8 (ebook)
     1. Reading (Elementary) 2. Education—Standards—United States. I. Title.
  LB1573.D577   2014
  372.4—dc23

  2014018099

     ISBN 978-0-8077-5590-7 (paper)
     ISBN 978-0-8077-5591-4 (hardcover)
     ISBN 978-0-8077-7333-8 (ebook)

Printed on acid-free paper
Manufactured in the United States of America

21 20 19 18 17 16 15 14   8 7 6 5 4 3 2 1

To: Allen, Stephen, and Patrick

To: Megan, Christopher, Alyssa, Drew, Caitlin, Cameron, Elijah, and Benjamin

To: All the wonderful teachers whom we have had the privilege to associate and learn from as colleagues and friends, with gratitude.

Contents

Foreword

Reading Across Multiple Texts in the Common Core Classroom, K–5 is the book for which elementary school literacy educators have been waiting for ever since the Common Core State Standards were released, simply because it clearly lays out how Standards 7 and 9 can and should be addressed in the classroom. Standard 7 requires students to integrate and evaluate content presented in diverse media and formats; Standard 9 requires students to analyze how two or more texts address similar themes and topics in order to build knowledge and understand a variety of approaches employed by authors. These two standards have opened new vistas for classroom educators that go beyond the comprehension of a single text.

Reading Across Multiple Texts clearly delineates what skills and strategies from past research and theory on literacy can be utilized and what new skills and strategies must be forged. Core features of this book include classroom-tested examples of successful lessons developed and taught by the authors. The book is a nice balance between focused insights on the part of the authors and clear actions to take as a result of those insights.

Early on in the book, the authors note that reading multiple texts on similar topics is not a new idea, but it has received its rightful place in the spectrum of literacy instruction only recently. Typically, when students are asked to read across multiple texts, they tend to read each text in isolation without making connections. Hence, the need for instructional practices for comparing and contrasting multiple texts—hence the need for this book.

The authors explain that texts come in a variety of types and formats. This makes the selection of texts that are appropriate to compare and contrast a critical aspect of planning. Pairing texts may be based on similar themes or topics, the author or illustrator, and on organization and presentation. To this end, the authors provide a planning template to make decisions as to what and how to compare.

Given the centrality of narrative texts in elementary education, the authors address it in depth. Narrative texts describe human experience and, thus, have a natural appeal to students of all grade levels. They follow a predictable format or structure that includes characters, setting, and plot. The authors remind us that as students progress through the grades, they encounter more complex and nuanced forms of narrative texts. With increased demands on students for integrating and comparing/contrasting information across complex texts, teachers should scaffold instruction by incorporating a variety of strategies that include graphic organizers, story maps, asking text-dependent questions, supporting answers with evidence from the text, and scanning for information.

Informational texts are treated in depth in *Reading Across Multiple Texts*. The authors note that these texts provide information and are generally more difficult to read than narrative ones due to lack of familiarity to many students, the preponderance of new vocabulary that denotes specific concepts, and varied types of text structures commonly not familiar to students. The authors emphasize the fact that knowing the various structures found in informational texts helps students identify the main idea and its details. Informational texts also include those presented digitally and graphically. As with narrative texts, students benefit by applying strategies like graphic organizers that match the structure of the text, including question/answer; sequence; cause and effect; problem/ solution; and compare/contrast. Other strategies include answering text-dependent questions of varying levels, summarizing texts, self-questioning, and researching information from online resources.

While the book contains a wide variety of strategies that can be taught to and used by students, the authors underscore the fact that a fundamental goal of literacy education is to build the background knowledge of students. The relationship between background knowledge and reading comprehension is reciprocal—the more one knows about a topic, the better the comprehension of the same topic; the more one reads about the topic, the more one knows. The authors continually remind us that while knowledge and strategies are both important, a strong knowledge base can make up for a lack of strategies, but strong strategies cannot make up for a lack of knowledge.

The stated purposes of *Reading Across Multiple Texts* are to demonstrate why students need to read across multiple texts, to provide strong examples of sets of these texts' lessons at primary and intermediate grade levels, and to present teaching and learning strategies that support multiple texts. The book accomplishes these purposes quite well along with others not explicitly stated. All K–5 literacy educators can benefit from this very thoughtfully written elucidation of a complex topic.

—Robert J. Marzano,
CEO, Marzano Research Laboratory

Preface

In this 21st-century society, we are constantly being besieged with information coming at us from all different directions. We read and hear news from TV, from magazines and newspapers, and, increasingly, from the Internet. We read and hear about current issues—from the latest weight-loss programs to the benefits of eating blueberries every day, from the latest cancer news to the overfishing of the oceans. The news and information bombard us at times, often with conflicting reports and glaring inconsistencies.

What to do with all this information? Sometimes we just want to learn everything we can about a topic. So the more we read, the more we learn about that topic. We may read several different Internet sources to learn more about a particular country we plan to visit. Other times, we may want to compare and contrast different sources of information or different ideas. We may want to read what different consumer reports say about a particular product we want to purchase. In order to do this, we may read multiple sources.

Still other times, we may want to hear alternative sides of a story or issue. For example, if we want to know about a certain medical procedure, we may want to hear all sides of the issue. We may seek out information about the benefits as well as drawbacks of this medical procedure so that we can make up our minds about the value of the procedure. If we want to know more about the use of drones, we may seek out both positive and negative views. We may want to hear from politicians and critical news analysts who favor and critique America's use of them around the world. Further, we may want to hear about the use of drones within the United States—the benefits as well as the drawbacks.

As the world grows ever more complicated, students need to become skillful at reading multiple sources, comparing, contrasting, and integrating texts. This necessity is addressed by the Common Core State Standards (CCSS), and the needed instruction for success is the topic of this book, *Reading Across Multiple Texts in the Common Core Classroom, K–5*. Reading across multiple texts refers to situations where an individual reads two or more texts, including those found on the Internet, to build knowledge, to compare or contrast ideas, to read or hear another viewpoint, or to resolve differences in ideas and issues.

Teachers want and need to know more about how to teach students to read across multiple texts. This skill is a critical part of the Reading Standards in the Common Core State Standards (www.corestandards. org), which were adopted in 45 of the 50 states, District of Columbia, 4 territories, and the Department of Defense Education Activity. In addition, reading across multiple texts is one new feature of the CCSS assessments. Both Smarter Balanced (www.smarterbalanced.org) and the Partnership for Assessment of Readiness for College and Careers (PARCC) (www.parcconline.org/parcc-assessment) include tasks that ask students to read more than one text and combine information from these texts. The National Assessment of Educational Progress (NAEP) has included this task for the last 2 decades (www.nces.ed.gov/nation-sreportcard).

This text focuses specifically on Reading Standards 7 and 9 of the CCSS (in bold in Figure P.1). Both of these standards ask students to read, think about, discuss, and write using multiple texts. These two standards are among the most complex of the CCSS and require deep understanding of and thinking about more than one text.

PRINCIPAL FEATURES OF THIS BOOK

Reading Across Multiple Texts in the Common Core Classroom, K–5 is intended as a practical guide for teachers. Classroom-tested examples of successful lessons developed and taught by the authors and professional colleagues are a core feature of the book and support three important purposes:

- To show why students need to learn to read across multiple texts,
- To provide strong examples of sets of multiple text lessons at the primary and intermediate grade levels, and
- To present teaching and learning strategies that support reading across multiple texts.

SCOPE OF THE BOOK

Each chapter provides a foundation for understanding a particular aspect of how to teach reading across multiple texts. Chapter 1 provides a rationale for why we want to teach our students to read, think about, critique, and evaluate multiple texts. It also includes a theoretical foundation and research that examines what students typically do when asked to read multiple texts on their own. Have you heard of the "accumulate and dump" approach? Research tells us that, when left to their own devices, most students take the accumulate and dump approach

Figure P.1. Reading Anchor Standards for the CCSS

ANCHOR STANDARDS FOR READING

Key Ideas and Details

1. Read closely to determine what the text says explicitly and to make logical inferences from it; cite specific textual evidence when writing or speaking to support conclusions drawn from the text.
2. Determine central ideas or themes of a text and analyze their development; summarize the key supporting details and ideas.
3. Analyze how and why individuals, events, and ideas develop and interact over the course of a text.

Craft and Structure

4. Interpret words and phrases as they are used in a text, including determining technical, connotative, and figurative meanings, and analyze how specific word choices shape meaning or tone.
5. Analyze the structure of texts, including how specific sentences, paragraphs, and larger portions of the text (e.g., a section, chapter, scene, or stanza) relate to each other and the whole.
6. Assess how point of view or purpose shapes the content and style of a text.

Integration of Knowledge and Ideas

7. **Integrate and evaluate content presented in diverse media and formats, including visually and quantitatively, as well as in words.**
8. Delineate and evaluate the argument and specific claims in a text, including the validity of the reasoning as well as the relevance and sufficiency of the evidence.
9. **Analyze how two or more texts address similar themes or topics in order to build knowledge or to compare the approaches the authors take.**

Range of Reading and Level of Text Complexity

10. Read and comprehend complex literary and informational texts independently and proficiently.

---

to reading multiple texts. They also select the largest text as the text with the most and best resources. (You'll read more about this in Chapter 1.) This chapter also discusses the implications of the research on reading across multiple texts, both of which can serve teachers as they move from the sample units of this text to creation of their own. Finally, this chapter will address and answer the question many teachers have about the CCSS: "What ever happened to strategic reading? Is it now gone, too?"

Chapter 2 examines the specific grade-level literacy and informational standards of Reading Anchor Standards 7 and 9 and shows what students are expected to know and be able to do to meet those standards. We show how primary- and intermediate-grade trade books can be used to provide examples of the use of the standards. Next, a primary-grade example of lessons shows how to teach kindergartners and 1st-graders to compare and contrast three versions of the same nursery rhyme, *Over in the Meadow*. The chapter also introduces a template that teachers can use to help plan and organize lessons around many texts.

Chapter 3 is a "how-to" chapter. It discusses three important preliminary issues: (1) What is a text? (2) What are different ways to combine texts together? and (3) How do you use the template introduced in Chapter 2 to develop lessons with multiple texts? Novice teachers want to know how to, and this chapter answers that important question. It provides step-by-step instructions for development of sets of lessons around a topic, theme, person, or issue.

Chapter 4 specifically addresses the nature of literary (or narrative) texts and why they are so important. Examples of two sets of lessons, one for primary-grade and one for intermediate-grade narrative texts, are organized around the template presented in Chapter 2. Following these lessons are several reading strategies that can be taught to students to support their success in meeting Standards 7 and 9 for narrative texts. These strategies include helping students answer text-dependent questions, helping them find evidence in a text, and helping them scan for information. Offline and online tools and supports complete the chapter.

Chapter 5 follows the organization of Chapter 4 using informational instead of literary texts. First, the chapter looks at why informational texts are hard for students to understand. Specific examples of sets of lessons for primary- and intermediate-grade informational texts provide models for teaching students to read across these texts. What is especially helpful in this chapter are the many and varied digital tools that can be used to support the teaching of the topics presented, butterflies for young readers and the *Titanic* survivors for older readers. These digital supports extend the concepts and ideas presented in the lessons to help students develop a deep understanding of them. Then a variety of instructional strategies are suggested for helping students understand and learn from informational texts. Most teachers have seen these instructional strategies in other settings, but here they will be applied to reading across multiple informational texts.

Chapter 6 addresses the important issue of reading to build knowledge, one of the important goals of Standards 7 and 9. The chapter stresses the development of deep knowledge of the topics students read about. It also directly addresses the question of: Do we teach for knowledge or strategies? The answer may be surprising. The chapter offers primary- and intermediate-grade sets of lessons designed to build students' knowledge of spiders at the primary-grade level and tsunamis at the intermediate-grade level. The chapter continues the emphasis on multimedia—especially from the Internet—for developing depth of knowledge of topics. It looks at the reciprocal relationship between developing background knowledge to prepare for reading texts and reading texts to expand background knowledge.

The book concludes with final thoughts on the importance of a variety of texts—from verbal to graphic to illustrative to print—for both literary and informational texts of various levels of complexity. It also concludes with a few principles or rules of thumb to think about when working with multiple texts.

INTENDED AUDIENCES OF THE BOOK

This book is designed to be useful to all educators who are concerned with helping K to grade 5 students grow in their abilities to read across multiple texts. Preservice elementary teachers and professors of education studying the reading standards of the CCSS can use the book as a supplement to other main texts in their reading and literacy methods classes. Preservice teachers will find the model lessons particularly useful as a way to think about and begin their own teaching of multiple texts.

The new teacher or one who has not been exposed to practices for having students read across multiple texts will gain the foundational knowledge needed to understand why this is important and to develop lessons using or adapting those in this book. Inservice teachers will find the book useful to supplement their knowledge and understanding of the standards in courses for the reading endorsement. The book will also help inservice teachers increase their skills in teaching students to make distinctions, integrate and evaluate information and sources, and form judgments based on multiple texts.

Reading and literacy coaches will find additional useful ideas and resources to integrate into their existing work. Additionally, there is much food for thought on the balance between developing background knowledge to aid text comprehension and using multiple texts to build background knowledge. There is also much information on how to teach students to reference specific texts in support of answers and positions. These skills are useful to literacy coaches as well as CCSS coaches who are helping teachers integrate literacy and disciplinary learning.

Finally, Professional Learning Communities (PLCs) of teachers will find the book useful as they delve more deeply into the reading standards of the Common Core. They can use *Reading Across Multiple Texts in the Common Core Classroom, K–5* as a point of discussion. Further, they can use the lessons in the book to begin or enhance their own teaching. They can use the text, lessons, and templates to evaluate and supplement the lessons in their core reading programs and/or develop new lessons.

For all educators, this endeavor to teach students how to read, think about, and critically analyze multiple texts will serve them well as readers throughout their lives.

CHAPTER 1

New Emphasis on Reading Across Multiple Texts

This chapter begins with some background on the use of reading across multiple texts in elementary classrooms today. Then comes a bird's-eye view of what research tells us (and does not tell us) about how well our students do when we ask them to read across multiple texts. Finally, the chapter examines how strategic reading applies to the new CCSS and particularly to reading across multiple texts.

LOOKING AT ELEMENTARY CLASSROOM PRACTICE

Up until the late 1990s, teaching one text at a time was common teaching practice in core reading materials and in most American elementary classrooms. Further, in most commercial standardized K–5 reading tests, students almost always answered questions about a single text. So the idea of teaching students to read across several texts was a fairly unfamiliar one to many teachers.

In the late 1990s, though, interest grew in reading across multiple texts, and resources to support it became available (Atwell, 1998; Calkins, 2010; Harvey & Goudvis, 2007). Units were built around reading across and writing about multiple texts. In addition, several authors have written about multigenre responses to literature (Gillespie, 2005; Romano, 2000), but these materials mostly come from a writing perspective rather than a reading perspective. In addition, these materials focus on secondary rather than elementary teachers and students.

In the core reading programs of the late 1990s and 2000s, publishers began to include a pairing of a literary text with an informational text, and students have been asked to think about the information in these texts. Most often, though, questions in the teachers' manuals of these core reading materials ask students to think about each text rather than to compare and contrast the information presented in both texts. Finally, some schools regularly ask students at the higher grade levels to compare and contrast the major characters in novels about similar themes—reading *The Cay* (Taylor, 2003), for example, and *Hatchet*

(Paulsen, 1987). But, by and large, reading across multiple texts has not been a common educational practice.

LOOKING AT THEORY AND THE RESEARCH

Even though we know that as adults we read multiple texts all the time—whether those texts are online or in magazines, books, or newspapers—the truth is that there is little research on the subject, possibly because it has taken time for the implications of the Internet-generated information explosion to be felt in our curricula and standards. This section describes what we do know from research as well as the theoretical underpinnings of the lesson development practices that follow in this text.

Sometimes practice-oriented teachers may prefer to skip the theory and move directly to the "how-do-I-do-it?" However, grounding in theory and research provides a useful guide through the decisionmaking of planning and implementing lessons. A good idea for a lesson lasts one day; a good theory lasts a lifetime. Further, research can help assess which teaching approaches are most likely to work. Research cannot give us all the answers, but it can guide us toward what is most likely to work for most students.

Cognitive and Situative Reading Comprehension

This book's theoretical framework for reading across multiple texts involves cognitive and situative models of reading and understanding text (Anderson, Greeno, Reder, & Simon, 2000). These models describe different aspects of educational processes that are fundamental to our understanding of reading and learning. A cognitive perspective on reading focuses on the individual and how the knowledge gained from reading is represented in an individual's mind. Kintsch's construction-integration model (2004) tells us that readers make two kinds of representations in their minds about what they read. Readers develop what he calls a "text-base" that is pretty much a basic understanding of a text. However, readers also develop what he calls a "situation-base" that is more in line with what the idea of the text is. Using as an example a sticky note with directions to get from where you are now to the nearest grocery store, the text-base would be the language of the directions itself—the specific words on the printed sticky note. The situation-base would be the mental picture in the reader's head of the spatial relations and markers (like shoe stores, a park, other buildings, etc.) between one's current location and the store. That mental picture represents the situation-base.

A situation-base understanding goes beyond just understanding the basic language of the text. A situation-base involves developing a mental model of the text (Johnson-Laird, 1989). To develop a mental model the reader must integrate the new information with background knowledge. In order to do this, the reader needs to know more than the surface level of the text. In the sticky note example, one needs to know the meaning of right and left, and understand basic measures of distance like blocks and miles or kilometers.

How is a cognitive perspective helpful for understanding reading across multiple texts? The perspective points out the importance of students' mental models of what they read. In order to read, understand, compare, contrast, and analyze texts, students are going to have to develop not just a text-base of what they read but a situation-base as well.

The situative perspective (not to be confused with "situation-base") also informs our understanding of reading across multiple texts. This perspective focuses on the social context in which reading and learning take place. This perspective sees reading as an interactive process between a reader and a text, and as such, it is an interactive and social as well as individual process (Brown, Collins, & Duguid, 1989). In addition, a situative perspective sees learning as embedded in the social practice of activities—for example, reading aloud to a group of students or reading in a small group. Each time a new activity takes place, a new learning takes place. Further, a situative perspective sees books, the Internet, and other reading materials as conceptual tools for learning. The more tools students use, the better they learn.

So, how does this perspective help us understand reading across multiple texts? In the common educational practices that we propose in this book, students gain from reading and learning in groups as much as from the individual activities that they do. In addition, the conceptual tools students use, including the many tools on the Internet, will help them process the information at a deeper level than they would otherwise.

What the Research Tells Us, and Where It Is Silent

What we do know from research on reading across multiple texts is that our students are not very good at it. It is important to note that so far, studies have not tried to teach students *how* to read across multiple texts. The research only looks at what students actually tend to do when we ask them to read across multiple texts on their own.

What Our Students Tend to Do. Goldman, her colleagues, and others (Goldman, 2004; Goldman, Meyerson, Wolfe, Mayfield, Coté, & Bloom,

1999; VanSledright & Kelly, 1998) examined what students do when asked to read multiple texts without the support or help of a teacher. These researchers found that students often take the "accumulate and dump" approach when they read more than one text in history. Their goal seems to be to gather the most information they can. They tend to treat each text by itself, with no connections to the other texts they are reading. Most often their verbal accounts of what they read contain bits of information without a combination of information. Further, they tend to treat each text uncritically. They don't engage in evaluation of the information in the texts, they don't integrate information from the different texts, and they don't integrate the information with their prior knowledge. They read one text in contented independence of the other text or their own background knowledge (Goldman, 2004).

When looking at two or more texts, intermediate and middle school students tend to see the most useful resource for gathering information as the one with the most information (Goldman et al., 1999). For example, when given a textbook and another text on a historical event, students tend to see the textbook as the best resource for understanding the event, regardless of the authenticity of the other text. Even if the other text is a diary, journal, or eyewitness account, the textbook will be viewed as the ultimate resource because it is most often the biggest text.

What Our Instruction and Assessments Do. Hartman (Hartman & Hartman, 1993; Hartman, 1995) argued that it is not surprising that students view reading as a single-text activity. After all, almost all instruction and assessment focus on the reading of a single text. From the beginning of basal reading programs in the 1940s and 1950s, instruction has been organized around the reading of a single text (Smith, 1965). Hartman provided the example of the before-, during-, and after-reading activities that have been and are still so prevalent in our elementary reading instruction. These activities are organized around the reading of a single text. Further, our assessments follow our instruction. And since instruction is organized around a single text, so are our reading assessments. Our assessments involve short reading passages in many different genres on many different topics. They do not allow students to examine a topic in depth and across different texts. As a result, students are cut off from connecting big ideas and information because they do not get opportunities to read across more than one text.

What Good Readers Do. Hartman (1995) conducted a relevant study that can help us understand better what it is that good readers do when they read across multiple texts. Hartman (1995) studied the reading of eight excellent high school readers. The students in Hartman's study were not typical students; their Preliminary Scholastic Aptitude Test scores were all above 91%. He had them think out loud as they read and processed five different online passages. Some of his findings are summarized here:

- Students used their background knowledge throughout the reading of multiple texts, not just before they read or early on in their reading.
- Students' understanding of a text was influenced by their reading of other texts, and their understanding of a given text often changed after reading other texts.
- Students did not process each text linearly but instead "zigzagged" through the texts, going back and forth with ideas and building a "mosaic of evidence" (p. 557).
- Students' critical reading appeared to be an open process that involved interpreting, examining evidence and internal logic, reinterpreting, and reevaluating ideas in the five texts they read.

The students in Hartman's study appeared to use many effective strategies for reading across multiple texts, and they appeared to be confident in doing so. We have all met students like these. However, most students need support and assistance to learn how to read across multiple texts, especially elementary students. It is the goal of this book to help you help them do this.

TEACHING STRATEGIC READING

Many teachers have noted that the new CCSS and new standards like reading across multiple texts have been bereft of any discussion about strategic reading. And yet, the reading field has spent years researching and demonstrating the importance of strategies for reading comprehension (for reviews see Dole, Nokes, & Drits, 2010; Kamil et al., 2008; Shanahan et al., 2010). We have learned the importance of teaching students to ask questions, summarize, predict, and use graphic organizers. In the new CCSS environment, many teachers have asked, "What happened to strategy instruction? We've spent the last decade on teaching students strategies. Now are we to abandon them?" This is an excellent question. The CCSS identifies what we want students to know and be able to do. Standards 7 and 9 tell us that students should be able to read across multiple texts in order to gain information about various themes or topics.

But the CCSS and Standards 7 and 9 are not curricula or instruction. The standards tell us what we want students to know and be able to do. The how-to in the "be able to do" is what strategy instruction is all about. Strategy instruction refers to the strategies that teachers teach and students use to be able to meet the standards. One of the most important ways we can show students how to be able to meet the standards related to multiple texts is through the strategic reading of texts. So, rather than abandon strategic reading, teachers still need to teach strategies to help students meet the standards. Each chapter of this book includes reading strategies to teach students to support their successful reading across narrative and informational texts.

SUMMARY

- ➢ Students' reading of multiple texts on similar topics and themes is not a new idea.
- ➢ Even with the availability of multiple texts on similar topics and themes, the instructional practice of comparing and contrasting multiple texts is not common.
- ➢ The limited research on reading across multiple texts indicates that when students are asked to read across multiple texts, they tend to read each text in isolation without making connections among the texts or with their own background knowledge.
- ➢ Students can be taught strategies that will help bridge these connections and build knowledge when reading across a variety of texts.

CHAPTER 2

Standards 7 and 9 of the CCSS

In Chapter 1 we presented some background information about the lack of classroom practice on reading across multiple texts and some theory and research about what students tend to do when asked to read multiple texts on their own. We also talked about strategic reading and how it fits into our instruction in reading across multiple texts.

In this chapter we first give you a broad overview of what Standards 7 and 9 tasks might look like and what students should be able to know and do. Then we present an example of the kind of lesson we suggest for reading across multiple texts.

READING STANDARDS 7 AND 9 FOR LITERATURE

What are students expected to know and be able to do to accomplish Reading Standards 7 and 9 for literary texts (Figures 2.1 and 2.2)? How can you assist students in accomplishing these reading standards for literature? Young children can begin by thinking about and comparing the illustrations in two literary texts that teachers have read aloud to them. For example, they think about how the illustrations in *George and Martha: The Best of Friends* (Marshall, 2011) and *Frog and Toad Are Friends* (Lobel, 2003) help them understand the stories better. They can discuss how the adventures of *George and Martha* and *Frog and Toad* are alike and how they are different. For kindergartners, teachers may have to prompt children's responses, perhaps by modeling the beginning of the answers for children. For example, "The characters of *George and Martha* and *Frog and Toad* are alike because they both . . ."

At the 2nd-grade level, students can compare and contrast the different illustrations of the fables and folktales they read or teachers read to them. Children can read similar folktales from different countries and compare how the authors changed characters or settings or other elements of the stories. Many teachers may be familiar with this particular activity and actually use it with their students because there is now a proliferation of fairy- and folktale books from other countries. Many of us have seen versions of *Cinderella* from different countries as well as humorous versions of *Goldilocks and the Three Bears* and *The Three Little Pigs*.

Figure 2.1. Grade-Level Standards for Standard 7 for Reading Literature

---

Kindergarten: With prompting and support, describe the relationship between illustrations and the story in which they appear (e.g. what moment in a story an illustration depicts).

Grade 1: Use illustrations and details in a story to describe its characters, setting, or events.

Grade 2: Use information gained from the illustrations and words in a print or digital text to demonstrate an understanding of its characters, setting or plot.

Grade 3: Explain how specific aspects of a text's illustrations contribute to what is conveyed by the words in a story (e.g. create mood, emphasize aspects of a character or setting).

Grade 4: Make connections between the text of a story or drama and a visual or oral presentation of the text, identifying where each version reflects specific descriptions and directions in the text.

Grade 5: Analyze how visual and multimedia elements contribute to the meaning, tone, or beauty of a text (e.g. graphic novel, multimedia presentation of fiction, folktale, myth, poem).

Figure 2.2. Grade-Level Standards for Standard 9 for Reading Literature

---

Kindergarten: With prompting and support, compare and contrast the adventures and experiences of characters in familiar stories.

Grade 1: Compare and contrast the adventures and experiences of characters in stories.

Grade 2: Compare and contrast two or more versions of the same story (e.g., Cinderella stories) by different authors or from different cultures.

Grade 3: Compare and contrast the themes, settings, and plots of stories written by the same author about the same or similar characters (e.g., in books from a series).

Grade 4: Compare and contrast the treatment of similar themes and topics (e.g., opposition of good and evil) and patterns of events (e.g., the quest) in stories, myths, and traditional literature from different cultures.

Grade 5: Compare and contrast stories in the same genre (e.g., mysteries and adventure stories) on their approaches to similar themes and topics.

By the 3rd grade, students are expected to move on to stories by the same author and examine closely how authors change their stories, their characters, their settings, and their plots. Students can explain in more detail how authors use the illustrations to add to the readers' understanding of characters, tone, or setting. Some teachers have built elaborate units for students to study an individual author and/or illustrator and the various stories and books the author or illustrator has created. Students can then compare and contrast the various elements and illustrations of those stories to examine more closely an author's craft. We have seen exceptional primary-grade studies of the works and illustrations of Leo Lionni, Ezra Jack Keats, Eric Carle, and Mo Willems.

By the 4th grade, students move on to more difficult tasks. Students are expected to be able to read a printed text and see a film or video on the Internet on the same text. Students then can make connections between the printed text and the film or video. They can write about ways in which the printed text differs from the visual presentation. They can do this orally as well. In addition, students can examine different books, myths, and legends for themes and topics from different cultures. Students can compare two picture books such as the Zimbabwean folktale *Mufaro's Beautiful Daughters* (Steptoe, 1987) and the Zuni folktale *The Turkey Girl* (Pollock, 1996). Students can also compare two novels that explore themes of good and evil such as *The Lion, the Witch, and the Wardrobe* (Lewis, 1994) and *The Dark Is Rising* (Cooper, 1999). They can discuss the different viewpoints about good and evil and how these are the same or different in the different novels.

Finally, in 5th grade, students can look at multimedia elements to compare and contrast themes across the same or different genres. So, for example, students can examine two mystery stories or historical fiction books and write about the author's theme in each. Students can examine the ways in which two different authors develop themes around the Revolutionary War by comparing *My Brother Sam Is Dead* (Collier & Collier, 2005) with *The Fighting Ground* (Avi, 2009). All of these types of tasks revolve around strengthening students' abilities to accomplish Standards 7 and 9 for literary texts.

READING STANDARDS 7 AND 9 FOR INFORMATIONAL TEXT

The standards for informational text are not much different from the standards for literature, although some differences stand out (Figures 2.3 and 2.4). The biggest difference is that while the standards for literature mention characters, setting, plots, problems, solutions, and themes, the standards for informational texts mention information, illustrations, and other visuals such as charts, graphs, media, and knowledge-building about the topics of the texts.

Standards for informational texts expect young children to begin to identify illustrations, graphs, charts, and tables and to know what kind of information these elements of an informational text provide. Examples of texts at these early levels include *Frogs* (Gibbons, 1994), *Frog: See How They Grow* (DK Publishing, 2007), and *Time for Kids: Bees!* (Time for Kids, 2005), which combine short amounts of text with

Figure 2.3. Grade-Level Standards for Standard 7 for Reading Informational Texts

Kindergarten: With prompting and support, describe the relationship between illustrations and the text in which they appear (e.g. what person, place, thing or idea in the text an illustration depicts).

Grade 1: Use the illustrations and details in a text to describe its key ideas.

Grade 2: Explain how specific images (e.g. diagram, showing how a machine works) contribute to and clarify a text.

Grade 3: Use information gained from illustrations (e.g. maps, photographs) and the words in a text to demonstrate understanding of the text (e.g. where, when, why and how key events occur).

Grade 4: Interpret information presented visually, orally or quantitatively (e.g. in charts, graphs, diagrams, time lines, animations or interactive elements on webpages) and explain how the information contributes to an understanding of the text in which it appears.

Grade 5: Draw on information from multiple print or digital sources, demonstrating the ability to locate an answer to a question quickly or to solve a problem efficiently.

Figure 2.4. Grade-Level Standards for Standard 9 for Reading Informational Texts

Kindergarten: With prompting and support, identify basic similarities in and differences between two texts on the same topic (e.g., in illustrations, descriptions, or procedures).

Grade 1: Distinguish between information provided by pictures or other illustrations and information provided by the words in a text.

Grade 2: Compare and contrast the most important points presented by two texts on the same topic.

Grade 3: Distinguish one's own point of view from that of the author of a text.

Grade 4: Integrate information from two texts on the same topic in order to write or speak about the subject knowledgeably.

Grade 5: Integrate information from several texts on the same topic in order to write or speak about the subject knowledgeably.

close-up photographs to support the text. Children at the K–2 grade level can begin to identify the difference between an illustration drawn by an illustrator and a photograph taken by a photographer. By the time students reach 3rd grade the standards for informational texts expect students to learn how to identify an author's viewpoint and to differentiate what the author says from what the student knows and understands. At this time, students are also expected to identify similarities and differences between two texts on the same topic.

At the 4th- and 5th-grade levels, the standards for informational text expect students to be able to interpret information presented in different media such as charts, graphs, timelines, or interactive elements on a webpage. They should be able to draw from multiple print and digital sources to build a knowledge base about a topic. Fourth-grade students can build knowledge of the solar system by reading two of the following informational books: *13 Planets: The Latest View of the Solar System* (Aguilar, 2011), *The Solar System* (Walsh, 2013), *Solar System: A Journey to the Planets and Beyond* (Graham, 2009), and *Our Solar System* (Simon, 2007). Fifth-grade students might develop a written report and an oral presentation about aspects of the Civil Rights Movement by reading Russell Freedman's (2008) *Freedom Walkers: The Story of the Montgomery Bus Boycott*, McWhorter's (2004) *A Dream of Freedom,* and Bausum's (2005) *Freedom Riders*. All of these types of tasks and activities focus students' attention on the specific elements of informational text that make it unique and quite different from the stories they are used to reading.

Taking into consideration the CCSS Reading Standards 7 and 9 and the kinds of tasks students are expected to accomplish, the lessons included in this book offer practical implementation of the ideas in the book through model lessons for K–5 classrooms. Chapters 4 and 5 are organized around literary and informational texts, consistent with the CCSS. Chapters 4, 5, and 6 all include sets of lessons at the primary-grade levels, either K–1 or 2–3 and at the intermediate grade levels, grades 4–5. For the lesson in this chapter, which is intended to introduce the model, however, we present a set of K–1 lessons only.

PRIMARY-GRADE LITERARY EXAMPLE

What might a series of lessons look like that would fit Standards 7 or 9 for literary texts (see Figure 2.5)? Here we provide an example of several lessons that Mrs. Trellor taught to her 1st-graders. She was interested in having her students think about and compare and contrast the approaches different authors and illustrators take on the same nursery rhyme, *Over in the Meadow*.

Figure 2.5. *Over in the Meadow* Template

	Text 1: *Over in the Meadow* (Keats, 1971)
	✓ Literary ☐ Informational
	Text 2: *Over in the Meadow* (Wadsworth, 2002)
	✓ Literary ☐ Informational

Figure 2.5. *Over in the Meadow* Template (continued)

	Text 3: Over in the Meadow (McDonald, 2011) ✓ Literary ☐ Informational	
Planning	***Grade-Level Standards*** (Lesson Objective): Use illustrations and details in a story to describe its characters, setting, or events. Compare and contrast similar texts written by different authors and illustrated by different illustrators.	
	Writing Prompt Question: How are the words and illustrations the same and different in three different books titled *Over in the Meadow*?	
	Strategy: Compare and contrast information that is similar and different in multiple texts.	
Text Analysis	*Similar*	*Different*
	Same title	
	Same animals in both books: • Birds-bluebirds • Turtle-dig • Bee • Crow • Fish • Frog • Lizard-bask	Different animals in each book: • Owls • Beaver • Muskrat • Cricket • Duck • Fireflies • Lizards are different colors
Writing	***Text/Sentence Frame*** (scaffolded response to writing prompt): Students will respond <u>orally</u> to a partner. "One way these books are the same is _____. One way these books are different is _____."	

LESSON—OVER IN THE MEADOW

Grades K–1

TEXT 1   Keats, E. J. (1971). *Over in the Meadow*. New York, NY: Penguin.

1. Read objectives with students. Tell them that they will read three books with the same title but that each book was written and illustrated by a different author and illustrator. Explain that they will compare and contrast books by telling how the words and illustrations are the same or different.

2. Build background knowledge. Display the word "meadow" along with a variety of pictures of meadows and ask: Does anybody know what a meadow is? What kinds of animals do you think you might find in a meadow? If children do not know what a meadow is, do a Google search of pictures of meadows to show children. Talk about the essential features of meadows.

3. Show children the cover of the book and read the title and names of the author and illustrator. Explain that this book is a nursery rhyme.

4. Read aloud the nursery rhyme, encouraging the children to chime in as they are able to predict the rhyming. Reread the story and have the children chime in as they can.

After Reading

1. Go through the book again and point out how many baby animals are in each picture. Write on the whiteboard the different animals the children mention. Go back and see how many babies are mentioned with each animal. Make sure the children see the pattern—with each new animal introduced, one more baby. List the number of babies beside each animal.

2. Have students draw a picture of their favorite animal from the text and indicate the right number of babies as well.

TEXT 2   Wadsworth, O. A. (2002). *Over in the Meadow.* New York, NY: North-South Books.

1. Before reading: Show the book read to the children yesterday and ask them to recount the text. Reread the nursery rhyme. Have children hold up their animal pictures.

2. Introduce new text. Ask: Can anyone tell me what the title of this book is? Point out that the title is the same. Ask: Is the cover illustration the same? What is the difference?

3. Read the names of the authors and illustrators of both books and discuss how the names are different. Ask: Do you think that the pictures in the book will be different? Do you think the words will be different? Why or why not?

4. Hand out 3x5 cards—one to each child. On one side write "same" and on the other side write "different." Explain to the children that you are going to read the new book. As you read about each animal, have the children hold up the card indicating if the animal is the "same" or "different."

5. Read the text aloud. Show the pictures as you are reading. Ask periodically, "Are the words the same or different? Are the pictures the same or different?"

Comprehension Strategy Instruction: Compare and Contrast Texts

1. Make a T-chart on the whiteboard. Label the columns "same" and "different." Ask children how the two nursery rhymes are the same and chart their responses in the "same" column. Do the same for elements of the rhyme that are different (Figure 2.6).

2. Help the children understand why the words and illustrations might be different. Ask: Why do you think the authors used different animals and the illustrators drew different pictures? Emphasize that different meadows in different parts of the world might have different animals that inhabit them and that an author and illustrator can choose the animals they want to include in the book.

3. Review the two books by having the children tell a partner how the books are the same. Tell the students to begin their response with "One way these books are the same is _____." Ask the students to tell how they are different. Have them begin their response with "One way these books are different is _____."

    TEXT 3   McDonald, J. (2011). *Over in the Meadow*. Boston, MA: Barefoot Books.

4. Introduce the new book. Ask children to guess what the title of the book is. Ask: Is this by the same author and illustrator as the other two books we just read? Do you think the pictures will be the same and the words will be the same?"

5. Read the new book. Ask: "How are the words and pictures the same and different in this book compared to the other two books we read?" Discuss same and different animals that are in the new book. Discuss what is the same and what is different about the book.

6. Play the McDonald CD with the song. Have the children sing along. Show pictures of the book so they can see each page as they sing.

Writing Prompt

How are the words and illustrations the same and different in three different books titled Over in the Meadow?

Sentence Frame for *Over in the Meadow*

The three books we read called *Over in the Meadow* are the same and different. They are alike because _____. They are different because _____.

Figure 2.6. *Over in the Meadow* Charts

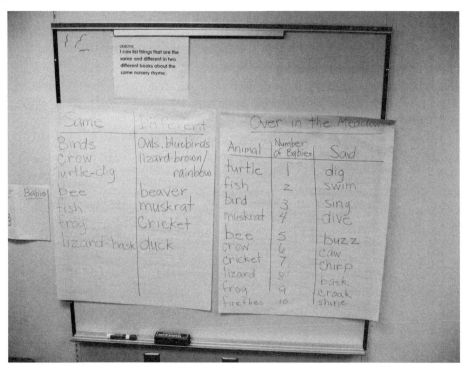

Over in the Meadow Extension

1. Tell the children that they will become authors and illustrators and make up their own *Over in the Meadow* nursery rhyme. To do this, begin by brainstorming a list of animals that might live in a meadow near them.

2. Use the following frame to complete a group rhyme. After deciding on the animal, help the students follow the patterns of baby animal numbers as well as the rhyming words.

    Over in the meadow where the _____ _____ _____

    lived a _____ _____ _____ and her little _____
    _____ (number).

    "_____," said the mother. "We _____," said the _____.

    So they _____ all day _____ _____ _____ _____
    _____.

SUMMARY

> ➢ Standards 7 and 9 of the CCSS for grades K–5 expect students to be able to analyze and learn from multiple texts of similar themes and topics.

> ➢ Teachers can select appropriate texts and provide instruction that supports students as they progress in their ability to analyze and learn from multiple texts.

CHAPTER 3

Choosing Texts and
Working Through the Template

This chapter looks at how to choose texts and work through the template to create lessons and activities to help students read and learn from multiple texts. The template is designed to be useful whether a teacher is using a core reading program or selecting texts independently, or a combination of the two.

CHOOSING TEXTS

To help students read across multiple texts, a teacher needs to choose appropriate texts for specific purposes. The selection of appropriate texts is a big hurdle that, once accomplished, makes the planning process much easier. When using a core reading program, texts will already be preselected. However, a teacher can supplement those texts with other texts and with instruction based on lessons included here.

A Broader Understanding of "Text"

We typically think of a text primarily as a textbook or some kind of picture book or novel. Or, we think of a text as a poem, a short passage, an article, or a newspaper piece. This book refers primarily to a text as a printed piece of work that has a linguistic structure. The *Merriam-Webster Dictionary* (http://www.merriam-webster.com/dictionary/text) defines a text as "the words that make up a piece of writing or speech." However, this book, aligned to the CCSS, helps teachers equip students to use many different media as texts, in addition to texts as historically understood, when exploring a theme, topic, person or issue. This expands our notion of what students can use as they gather information. They can (and should) use linguistic text—that is, print. But they can supplement these traditional texts with pictures, video, and online media. Consistent with a cognitive perspective, using many different media helps students develop a "situation-base" understanding of what they are reading rather than just a text-based understanding. Pictures, video, and online media help students develop mental models or pictures in their minds that complete and expand on their understanding of the printed words they read. Including visual media in addition to printed text is critically important when working with our underserved populations, our English language learners, and struggling readers.

Selecting Texts That Go Together

Hartman and Hartman (1993) present some interesting ways of combining texts that are integrated into the categories in the bulleted list below, all of which can help meet Standards 7 and 9 by enabling students to compare and contrast across many different kinds of texts as well digital and visual media.

- **Same author texts.** One way to combine texts is to select several texts by the same author. The example that Hartman and Hartman use is the trilogy that Maurice Sendak wrote, *Where the Wild Things Are* (1963), *In the Night Kitchen* (1970), and *Outside Over There* (1981). We don't often think of these books as connected, but Sendak himself suggests they can be studied together for similar illustrations, themes, and ideas (Cott, 1983). Studying several texts by the same author is one important approach that students can use to accomplish Standards 7 and 9. Other authors a teacher might use to help students to study the craft of one author include Leo Lionni, Jan Brett, Gary Paulson, and Kate DiCamillo.
- **Same literary texts.** Another approach that many teachers have taken is to read different versions of the same story. For 20 years or so, there have been different versions, and funny versions, of the old fairytales that have delighted primary- and intermediate-grade students. For example, students can read three versions of the same story: *Goldilocks and the Three Bears* (Marshall, 1998), *Goldilocks and the Three Bears* (Brett, 1992), and *Goldilocks and the Three Bears* (Buehner, 2009). Primary- and intermediate-grade students can compare and contrast the different versions of the stories, including the characters and their motives, attitudes, and beliefs, the different settings, and the different illustrations. Then students can read *Goldilocks and the Three Dinosaurs* (Willems, 2012), *Believe Me, Goldilocks Rocks! The Story of the Three Bears as Told by Baby Bear (The Other Side of the Story)* (Loewen & Avakyan, 2011), or *Goldilocks and the Three Bears: A Tale Moderne* (Guernaccia, 2010) for humorous, updated versions of the story and compare and contrast them with earlier, more traditional versions.
- **Same theme texts.** These texts explore a common theme. For example, several intermediate-grade level books can be used to

explore the theme of survival: *The Cay* (Taylor, 2003), *Island of the Blue Dolphins* (O'Dell, 1960), *Hachet* (Paulsen, 1987), *Holes* (Sachar, 2000), *Julie of the Wolves* (George, 2003), and *My Side of the Mountain* (George, 2004). All of these books address the theme of survival using different characters in different settings. Another theme that students can study is overcoming challenges by reading *Wonder* (Palacio, 2013), *Frindle* (Clements, 1996), *Sugar and Ice* (Messner, 2010), and *Each Little Bird That Sings* (Wiles, 2005). Once again, the characters, settings, and timelines change in these texts, but the overarching theme of overcoming obstacles ties them together.

- **Same person texts.** Another way to think about combining books is to read multiple texts about the same person. For example, students can read both literary and informational books to learn more about Frederick Douglass (*Frederick Douglass: The Last Day of Slavery*, Miller, 1996; *Frederick Douglass: Abolitionist Hero*, Stanley, 2008; *A Picture Book of Frederick Douglass*, Adler, 2005 [book and CD included]; *Words Set Me Free: The Story of Young Frederick Douglass*, Cline-Ransome, 2012). Each text provides different information about Frederick Douglass, and, by combining the books, students get a fuller picture of Douglass and what he stood for.

- **Same topic texts.** A common way of combining texts is to select several texts on the same topic—interesting topics in science like tsunamis and earthquakes—or topics in social studies like Native Americans or the history of different states. Grouping a set of texts helps students learn more about a topic of interest to them. In this book we present examples of texts that tell the story of tsunamis and the devastation they can create. By way of reading multiple texts, students can develop deep knowledge about different topics and write and speak knowledgeably about those topics—consistent with Standard 9.

- **Same craft or structure texts.** A final way that texts can be combined is by the same craft or structure. This combination could be used when examining authors who use similar structures such as the series of informational books including Moore's *If You Lived at the Time of the Civil War* (1994) and *If You Lived at the Time of the American Revolution* (1998) or Levine's *If You Traveled on the Underground Railroad* (1993) and *If You Traveled West in a Covered Wagon* (1992). Each of these texts is structured similarly in a question/answer format. Uchida wrote several texts based on her experiences as a young woman in the World War II Japanese Internment Camp at Topaz, Utah, including a historical fiction novel, *Journey to Topaz* (1984), a picture book, *The Bracelet* (1996), and her personal memoir, *The Invisible Thread* (1995). These texts can be studied through an examination of the author's craft.

Using the Template

Once a teacher has selected texts, then a set of lessons can be developed using the template. Figure 3.1 presents a blank template.

The Six-Step Template

This section walks though the six-step template and shows how to think about and plan materials and activities using the template.

Step 1: List the texts you will use. Also think about the other materials you will use. What visuals and online resources will further and deepen your students' thinking? Thinking about these texts will help you determine strategies to teach students so they learn from the multiple texts they read.

HINT: To find texts on the same topic, theme, person, or issue, use the Internet. Amazon.com is a great resource. Just type in the topic, theme, person, or issue (e.g., children's books on volcanoes), and up will come a set of related children's books. Also, you can just do a Google search on "volcanoes" to retrieve many wonderful visuals and multimedia sources.

Step 2: What is the lesson objective? This should come from your grade-level standard that you would like students to work on.

Step 3: What are the reading and writing strategies that your students will need to select and use in order to accomplish the grade-level objective or standard? Will students need to be able to scan for information to find the key ideas and details? Will they need to be able to write summaries or synthesize information from two or more texts? Whatever strategies are needed to accomplish the standard should be taught and/or reviewed sometime during the lessons.

Step 4: In the boxes across from "Text Analysis" record the specific information you want your students to glean from the readings and discussion. This step is really the heart of the template. Your activities will be selected depending on the objectives of your lesson. For example, you may want to have your students compare and contrast themes in different novels or picture books. You may want to combine information from three different texts on the same topic. You may want to develop a graphic organizer to compare and contrast how authors alter a traditional fairytale's ending.

Step 5: Across from the Writing Box is a space for a Text/Sentence Frame. This is a set of complete sentences with missing words and phrases

Figure 3.1. Blank Template

	Text 1: ☐ Literary ☐ Informational
	Text 2: ☐ Literary ☐ Informational
Planning	*Grade-Level Standard* (Lesson Objective):
	Writing Prompt Question:
	Strategy:

	Similar	*Different*
Text Analysis		

Writing	*Text/Sentence Frame* (scaffolded response to writing prompt):

that students fill in. The sentences provide the overall organization or structure for a response to a writing prompt. At the end of the set of lessons, the writing prompt asks a question that students will answer to show that they have achieved the objective of your lesson. For example, if the objective is to compare and contrast how authors alter a fairytale's ending, then the writing prompt should require students to compare and contrast the endings of the books they read. This way, you will be able to see directly if students can meet the objective. The Text/Sentence Frame helps students begin this process of writing to a prompt. The Frame is a scaffold to be removed after students have written many responses and know the general structure of a written response to a prompt. The scaffold is an excellent way to differentiate instruction. Some students, English language learners, perhaps, or struggling readers, may need the scaffold longer than others.

    A Flexible Template: The template is flexible in that you can think about the grade-level standards broadly and holistically. These grade-level standards are ways of thinking about how to scaffold experiences for students as they progress through the grades, K–5. But they are not set in stone. Thus, you may want to introduce students to some experiences and activities that are a year below their particular grade level and/or above their grade level. Students will benefit from this, and it may make it easier for you to plan.

SUMMARY

> ➤ Texts come in a variety of types and formats. Selecting the appropriate text for a specific purpose is critical in the planning process.
>
> ➤ Pairing texts may be based on content (similar theme or topic), author and/or illustrator, or organization and presentation.
>
> ➤ The template presented in this chapter provides a framework for planning lessons using multiple texts.
>
> ➤ Lesson components to consider include the topic or theme and what you plan to do with it, a list of texts and related materials, the lesson objective, strategies to support student learning, reading activities that are aligned with the lesson objective, and a writing response.

CHAPTER 4

Reading Across Multiple Literary Texts

This chapter focuses on one kind of literary texts—narrative texts. It discusses the important elements of narratives and shows how to teach students to read across multiple narrative texts. It offers examples of lessons wherein students read to compare and contrast elements of these texts. It also shows how to teach students the strategies they need to complete the tasks expected of them in Standards 7 and 9 of the CCSS for reading literature. Multiple digital, video, and audio presentations are suggested as supplemental "texts" that will help students build a deeper understanding of the texts they read, thereby enabling them to develop a situation-base of the concepts and topics across multiple texts.

NARRATIVE VERSUS LITERARY TEXTS

This chapter focuses only on narrative texts, not on all literary texts. An area of confusion for many teachers is the difference between narratives and literary texts. One reason for confusion is that the literacy field itself defines these terms in many different ways (see, for example, Duke, 2000; the National Assessment of Educational Progress [National Assessment Governing Board, 2011]). The CCSS (2010) offers the following definition: "Literary texts refer to different genres within thematic categories that contain literary features." Poems, short stories, fables, and even essays could be considered literary texts if they contains literary features (National Assessment Governing Board NAEP Framework, 2013). Literary text genres come in many different forms (see Figure 4.1). *Over in the Meadow*, for example, is a literary text that rhymes, but it is not a narrative text.

Narratives are a particular kind of literary text that follows a certain organization or structure (National Assessment Governing Board NAEP Framework, 2013). This structure is quite familiar to all of us. Narratives have a setting, characters, and a plot that consists of a problem and events that lead to the resolution of the problem. This distinction is an important one, since the purpose here is to show how to help students read across narrative texts using a story structure. The next section looks at why this is so important for students' reading growth.

Figure 4.1. Examples of Literary Text Genres

Plays	Myths	Classic Literature
Short Stories	Legends	Novels
Folktales	Tall Tales	Historical Fiction

WHY ARE NARRATIVE TEXTS SO IMPORTANT?

What do narrative texts have in common? Graesser, Golding, and Long (1991) proposed that the distinctive and identifying characteristic of a narrative is that it has a "chain of events"—things that happen in a certain predictable chronological order. Chains of events are familiar to everyone within our culture because they are part of our life experiences. For example, a common experience of adults is to drive to the grocery store and park the car. It is all too possible in this moment to be thinking about the shopping list and, in a moment of orientation toward shopping rather than the task at hand, to open the car door, get out, and instantly realize that the keys are still in the car and the car locked. The driver in this story is now locked out of the car and must call a locksmith to unlock it. The driver calls the locksmith and tells the location. The locksmith arrives and uses his tools to unlock the car. After the car is open, the driver pays the locksmith, thanks him, and decides whether or not there is still time to buy groceries.

In fact, this little scenario represents a story. There are characters, a setting in which the story takes place, a problem that occurs, and a chain of events that unfolds and leads to a resolution to the problem at the end. In addition, the characters in our story have feelings and emotions that we can relate to (Have you ever locked yourself out of your car?), and the setting of the story takes place somewhere we know very well (the parking lot of the grocery store we frequent). Problems and chains of events are experiences we all share as human beings (at one time or another, most of us have called locksmiths to open our car or house). Thus, the narratives we listen to or read are similar enough to the stories in our daily lives to give these narratives important familiarity and meaning.

The structure or organization of stories has a deep psychological reality to us as human beings (Graesser et al., 1991). Researchers describe our knowledge about stories as a specific kind of background knowledge we all have. Just as most young children have background knowledge about families and brothers and sisters, they also have background knowledge about how stories are structured or organized. These stories can be learned through TV and the media and, most importantly, from being read to.

The structure of stories, or story structure (Mandler & Johnson, 1977; Stein & Glenn, 1979), has long been known by reading researchers. Story structure consists of knowledge of the parts of stories—characters, settings, a problem, unfolding events, a resolution—and how those parts fit together (Figures 4.2 and 4.3). Young children develop a mental outline of stories in general. When they read a specific story, they use this outline to fill in missing information, to help them understand the feelings and motives of characters, and to follow the sequence of events in a story (Fitzgerald, 1989).

Our mental outline of narratives has been proven to be essential to comprehension. In fact, research indicates that both low-achieving and expert readers comprehend better when the text conforms to an organizational format, or story structure, that meets their expectations (Mandler & Johnson, 1977; Stein & Glenn, 1979). The familiar organization of narratives also helps readers predict, recall events, and focus attention (McConaughy, 1982). On the other hand, when narratives contain unfamiliar segments or an altered sequence, readers do not comprehend or remember as much (Graesser et al., 1991).

Due to the fact that the CCSS demands the use of more advanced and often complex narratives, elementary teachers are wise to pay close attention to students' knowledge of simple as well as more complex story structures. A basic understanding of a story structure is necessary but not sufficient for comprehension at the higher grade levels. As students move up the grades, they will likely need explicit instruction in the more complex structures of narrative texts.

Story Structure and Complex Texts

The CCSS stresses students' abilities to read and understand complex texts. The structure of narrative texts is an important part of text complexity. The more complex the structure of the text is, the more difficult it is to read and understand. Of course, other elements in stories, like language and knowledge demands, matter as well (CCSS, 2010). Texts are easier to understand when there are familiar language and content that students can relate to. For example, one reason why *Lilly's Purple Plastic Purse* (Henkes, 1996) is easy to understand is because Lilly is a primary-grade student and the story takes place in school. The text is written with familiar language, familiar content, and a simple and therefore familiar structure.

On the other hand, as students move to the intermediate grades, stories become more complicated, with less familiar structure and language and more knowledge demands. An example of this change is seen in the 2010 Newbery Medal winner *When You Reach Me* (Stead, 2009).

Figure 4.2. Primary-Grade Example of a Story Map

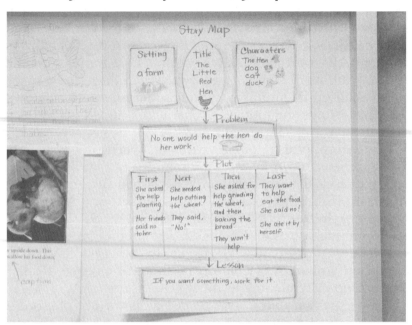

Figure 4.3. Intermediate Grade Example of a Story Map

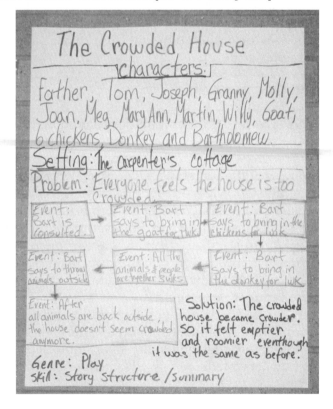

The multigenre structure of this text increases its level of complexity. The novel includes elements of mystery and suspense, science fiction, and historical fiction. There is more than one story line within this novel that takes place in New York City in the 1970s. Keeping the story lines straight, while simultaneously keeping track of clues woven throughout the text in order to solve the mystery, will be challenging for many intermediate-grade students. Although students will relate to common threads about a group of friends in the 6th grade, they may not understand some of the events and characters that are relevant to the 1970s. Miranda (the main character) lives in Manhattan with her mother, who is practicing to be a contestant on *The $20,000 Pyramid* hosted by Dick Clark. Miranda's favorite book is the Newbery Award winner *A Wrinkle in Time* (L'Engle, 1962). Stead makes frequent references to the book and the theme of time travel throughout *When You Reach Me*. Miranda receives a series of mysterious notes from someone who knows things that are going to happen before they happen. Students who are not familiar with *A Wrinkle in Time* or the notion of time travel may miss important clues that are woven throughout the text. In this story, and in other stories with multiple story lines, it is important for students to track the different story structures embedded in the larger story. This helps them focus on the specific story plots and the larger overall story structure as well.

Story Structure and Struggling Readers

The CCSS requires that students read complex texts like *When You Reach Me* (Stead, 2009). And while the structure of this novel and many like it may be difficult, the focus of the new standards is for teachers to provide scaffolding for students to read more of these complex texts.

To many students at the intermediate grade levels, the structure of stories is typically a well-established part of their understanding of stories. This is because these students have been read to from their early infant experiences to kindergarten and beyond. These children have hundreds, even thousands, of hours of hearing stories and talking about stories with their parents and caregivers. One of the lasting legacies of these experiences is a clear and strong understanding of how stories unfold. This helps children as they learn to read on their own.

On the other hand, children who have not been read to may have listened to and talked about stories for only a dozen or so hours (Adams, 1990). For these children, the structure of a story is not firmly embedded in their minds. With a deeper understanding of the structure of stories, these children's comprehension will improve. A classic study by Singer and Donlan (1982) provides evidence for this. In this study intermediate-grade students were taught to use a story structure to answer questions about narratives that they read. What researchers found was that lower-achieving readers' comprehension of narratives improved through the story structure questions and answers. Higher-achieving readers' comprehension did not improve. Singer and Donlan surmised that higher-achieving readers already had a deep understanding of story structure and therefore were not helped by the strategy. Lower-achieving readers, on the other hand, likely did not have such a deep understanding of narratives and therefore were helped by the strategy.

The Special Role of Vocabulary

Vocabulary plays a special role in narrative texts. Hiebert (2011) describes this special role as one of carrying nuanced meanings within narrative texts and their story elements. Vocabulary in narrative texts typically includes many unique rare words that convey the complexity and depth of the story. For example, a primary-grade selection might include words like "amazing" for very good, "enormous" for large, and "clustered" for grouped together. These words reflect the nuanced meanings that the author intends to convey (Figure 4.4).

Hiebert (2011) as well as Armbruster and Nagy (1992) have argued that there are significant differences between the words found in

Figure 4.4. Primary-Grade Vocabulary Board

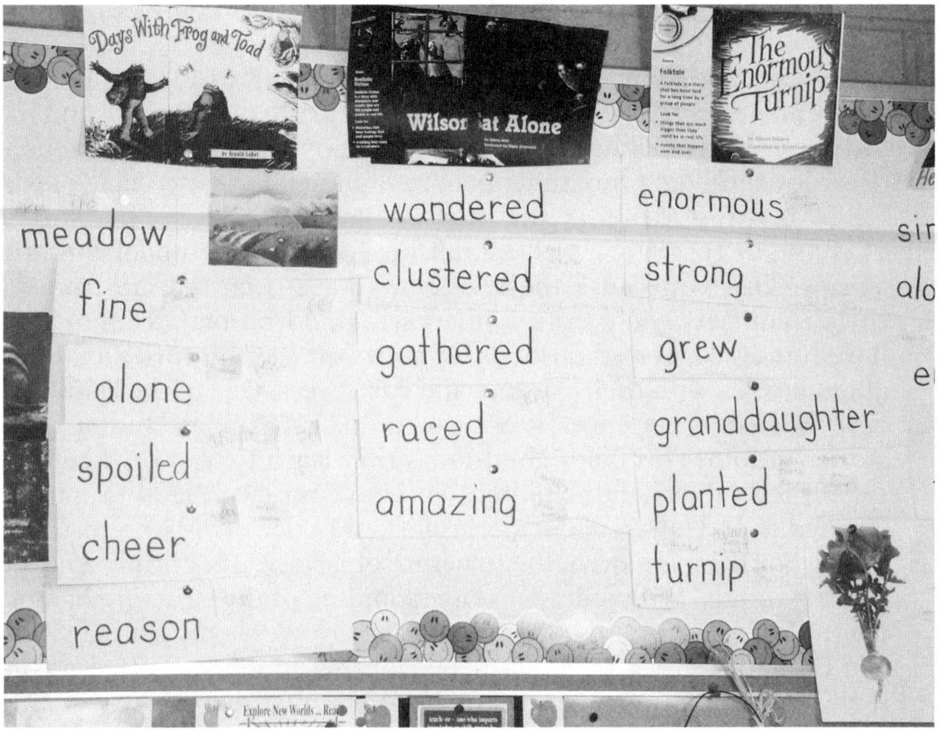

narrative and informational texts. While informational texts consist of many words related to specific content areas, narrative texts do not. Despite what many people may think, narratives often consist of more rare words than do informational texts. In addition, rare words in informational texts are repeated, whereas rare words in narrative texts are not. For example, if an author of an informational text uses the word "ecosystem," that word will be used throughout the text. On the other hand, an author of a narrative text will often vary the words used for a specific character trait. A narrative author may substitute *fright, trepidation, horror, fearfulness,* and *panic* for *terror*. Each nuanced word means something a bit different, and authors of narrative texts use these words as part of their craft.

So even if some of the content of a narrative text is familiar to students, they still might be flummoxed by so many new and unfamiliar words. Of course, encountering some unknown words should present few problems for readers. However, there comes a tipping point where there are so many unknown words that the story ceases to make sense.

PRIMARY-GRADE NARRATIVE EXAMPLE

This chapter's example of a primary-grade set of lessons across multiple narrative texts links to the Grade 2–3 Reading Literature, Standard 7, read as RL2.7 and Reading Literature, Standard 9, read as RL2.9 (see Figure 4.5). These standards provide a unique way of helping children see how authors and illustrators change different aspects of the same texts—allowing them to study in depth and detail what makes the texts the same and what makes them different.

There are many wonderful adaptations of fairytales in children's books on the market now, and primary-grade as well as intermediate-grade students love to listen to them and read them. The selected texts here include *Goldilocks and the Three Bears* (Marshall, 1998) and its newest adaptation, *Goldilocks and the Three Dinosaurs* (Willems, 2012). The Willems adaptation is a delightful twist on the original (Figure 4.6). Students love the variation on the theme, and they enjoy the author's voice and clever illustrations that bring the fairytale up to the 21st century.

Figure 4.5. Second-Grade Standards 7 and 9: Reading Literature

Standard 7: Use information gained from the illustrations and words in a print or digital text to demonstrate understanding of its characters, setting, or plot.

Standard 9: Compare and contrast two or more versions of the same story (e.g., Cinderella stories) by different authors or from different cultures.

Figure 4.6. *Goldilocks* Template

	Text 1: Goldilocks and the Three Bears (Marshall, 1998) ✓ Literary ☐ Informational
	Text 2: Goldilocks and the Three Dinosaurs (Willems, 2012) ✓ Literary ☐ Informational
Planning	**Grade-Level Standards** (Lesson Objectives): **RL2.7** Use information gained from the illustrations and words in a print or digital text to demonstrate understanding of its characters, setting, or plot. **RL2.9** Compare and contrast two or more versions of the same story (e.g., Cinderella stories) by different authors or from different cultures.
	Writing Prompt Question: How are the two stories of Goldilocks the same and different?
	Strategy: Story map strategy, compare and contrast strategy

	Similar	*Different*
Text Analysis	• Goldilocks • Food, chairs, beds • Goldilocks runs out the door	• No baby • Different looks of Goldilocks • Bears and dinosaurs • Pudding–porridge • Breaking the chairs–too tall chairs • Goldilocks sleeps in Baby Bear's bed but not in the dinosaur's bed. • Bears didn't want Goldilocks in their home–dinosaurs set trap to eat Goldilocks.

Writing	***Text/Sentence Frame*** (scaffolded response to writing prompt): *Goldilocks and the Three Bears* is like *Goldilocks and the Three Dinosaurs* because both stories _____. They are also alike because both stories _____. They are different because in the *Goldilocks and the Three Bears* story, Goldilocks _____. But in the *Goldilocks and the Three Dinosaurs* story, Goldilocks _____.

LESSON—GOLDILOCKS

Grades 2–3

TEXT 1   Marshall, J. (1998). *Goldilocks and the Three Bears*. New York, NY: Penguin Group USA.

Prepare a chart of a blank story map to complete as you read the story.

1. Read the objectives with students. Tell students that they will read two stories about Goldilocks, just like in the story *Goldilocks and the Three Bears*. Each book has a different author and illustrator. Explain that they are going to compare and contrast both stories. Make sure to clarify what compare and contrast mean—students will think about how the stories are the same and different. They will also think about the illustrations of the stories and how these help them understand the characters and the plot.

2. Activate background knowledge. Ask: How many of you know the story of *Goldilocks and the Three Bears*? Remind students that they may be familiar with this story, but they may not be familiar with the illustrator, James Marshall. Point out the picture on the cover of the book of Goldilocks smiling and dancing on the stump of a tree as the three bears merrily ride a bicycle out of sight.

3. Read and discuss the story. Complete a story map (see Figure 4.2) as the book is read.

4. Possible questions to ask:

    a. Who is the main character of the story? What do we know about her so far?

    b. What should we write for the setting?

    c. What seems to be the problem in this story?

    d. How do the pictures in the story help you understand the characters, and what is happening in the story? What are the events that lead to the solution of the problem (plot)?

    e. How does the story end? What is the solution or the lesson?

After Reading

Have students use the story map to retell the story to a partner. Be sure to have students include a discussion of which and how the illustrations helped them understand the characters and the plot. Be sure to have students include the problem and the major events that lead to the resolution of the story.

TEXT 2   Willems, M. (2012). *Goldilocks and the Three Dinosaurs.* New York, NY: Balzer + Bray.

1. Read the objectives with students. Review the Goldilocks story they read yesterday by showing and verbally walking through the story map they jointly constructed the day before.

2. Introduce the new book title and author. Remind students that they are to be thinking about how the illustrations help readers understand the characters and what is happening in the story. They can use this information to help them think about how these two stories are the same and different.

3. Read and discuss the story. Complete the story map as the book is read aloud, silently, alone, with a partner, or as a group choral read.

4. Possible questions to ask:

    a. What do we know about the characters in this story? How do the illustrations help us understand the characters?

    b. Where does the story take place?

    c. What did the author mean by "One day *FOR NO PARTICULAR REASON*, the three Dinosaurs made up their beds, positioned their chairs just so, and cooked three bowls of delicious chocolate pudding *FOR NO PARTICULAR REASON*"?

    d. What are the Three Dinosaurs planning to do? Where do you find evidence to support your answer?

    e. What do you think Mama Dinosaur meant by, "I sure hope no innocent little succulent child happens by our unlocked home while we are… uhhh . . . someplace else?" Help students understand that in this text, the dinosaurs did have a particular reason—to set a trap for Goldilocks so they could eat her. Discuss what "succulent" means first. This will help students understand what the dinosaurs want.

5. Continue reading and charting the rest of the story. Ensure that students are following along and understanding the twist in the Willems text and how it differs from the familiar story of Goldilocks. In the familiar story Goldilocks happens to find the bears' house, but the bears meant no harm. On the other hand in the Willems text the dinosaurs are actually setting a trap for Goldilocks so they can eat her—"the delicious chocolate-filled-little-girl bonbons." It will also help to define "bonbons" for students.

After Reading

Review the story by completing a second story map of the Three Dinosaurs text.

Comprehension Strategy Instruction:
Compare and Contrast Narrative Texts

1. Display and review story maps of both books (see Figure 4.11).

2. At this point students may have superficial ideas about what is the same and different in both books. That is okay. Some students may also see the Dinosaur book as incorporating elements of both Goldilocks and Hansel and Gretel, and you can explore with them this comparison to yet another text. Students typically need a second read of the Willems book because it is more difficult, and there are some interesting twists to this book that 2nd- and 3rd-graders have a more difficult time identifying.

    a. Remind students that the purposes of this lesson are to (1) look at the illustrations and think about how they help us understand the story, and (2) compare and contrast how the two stories and the illustrations are alike and how they are different. Tell students that you will use the two story maps to figure out some ways the stories are alike and different.

3. Display a T-chart labeled "SAME" and "DIFFERENT."

4. Use the following questions to determine similarities and differences. Chart information.

    a. Let's talk about the illustrations. How do they help you understand the story better?

    b. What do you notice that is the same in both books? What is different?

    c. How are the problems and solutions in both stories different? Did the Bears want or expect Goldilocks to barge into their home? Did the Dinosaurs want or expect Goldilocks to barge into their home?" (Point out that the Dinosaurs had bad intentions of capturing and eating Goldilocks.)

    d. What happens to Goldilocks at the end of each story?

5. Refer to the template (Figure 4.6) for a list of possible items in the SAME and DIFFERENT columns.

Writing Prompt

How are the two stories of Goldilocks the same and different?

Use the story frame below to help students write a paragraph describing the similarities and differences of the two stories. Scaffold the writing as needed.

Goldilocks Sentence Frame

Goldilocks and the Three Bears is like *Goldilocks and the Three Dinosaurs* because both stories _____.

> They are also alike because both stories _____.
>
> They are different because in the *Goldilocks and the Three Bears* story, Goldilocks _____. But in the *Goldilocks and the Three Dinosaurs* story, the three dinosaurs _____.

INTERMEDIATE-GRADE NARRATIVE EXAMPLE

This next set of intermediate-grade lessons are designed to meet Reading Standard 7, read as RL4.7 and Reading Standard 9, read as RL4.9, first helping students with RL4.7, "make connections between the text of a story or drama and a visual or oral presentation of the text" (Figure 4.7), and then with RL4.9, "comparing and contrasting the treatment of similar themes and topics (e.g., opposition of good and evil) and patterns of events in stories, myths, legends and traditional literature from different cultures" (Figure 4.9).

LESSON—MANDARIN DUCKS AND THE SWEETEST FIG

Grades 4–5

TEXT 1   Paterson, K. (1990). *The Tale of the Mandarin Ducks*. New York, NY: Scholastic.

1. Read the objective with students. Tell students that the goal of this first lesson is to make connections between a printed text (show text) and an animated film that they will view about the same story on the Internet.
2. Generate background knowledge about when students have read books and then seen the same movie on TV or in the movie theater. Discuss the differences between reading a story and seeing a film or movie on the same story. How are they both alike? How are they different?
3. Now discuss an animated film and how it is different from a typical movie or film that students often see. Name different animated films they have seen.
4. Tell students that today they will read a Japanese story about two Mandarin Ducks. As they read the story, stop them periodically to complete a story map (Figure 4.8).
5. Possible questions to ask:
   a. What do we know about the Lord of the district? What evidence does the author provide to support the traits of the Lord of the district being

Figure 4.7. *Mandarin Duck* Template

Planning	**Text 1:** *The Tale of the Mandarin Ducks* (Paterson, 1990) ✓ Literary ☐ Informational **Text 2:** The Tale of the Mandarin Ducks http://video.nhptv.org/video/2238438897/ ✓ Literary ☐ Informational **Grade-Level Standard** (Lesson Objective): **RL4.7.** Make connections between the text of a story or drama and a visual or oral presentation of the text. **Writing Prompt Question:** What are the connections between the printed text and the animated film for *The Tale of the Mandarin Ducks*? **Strategy:** Students compare and contrast two different versions of the same Japanese story about the Mandarin Ducks.

	TEXT 1: Connections	**TEXT 2: Connections**
Text Analysis	• •	• •

Writing	**Text/Sentence Frame** (scaffolded response to writing prompt): Several connections can be made between the print text and the animated film of *The Tale of the Mandarin Ducks*. First, both the book and the film _____. Second, both the book and the film _____. However, there are also differences between the two texts. In the book, the illustrations show _____. In the animated film, the illustrations show _____. The _____ is better than the _____ because _____.

mean and cruel? Draw students' attention to the idea that the lord of the district wanted to be surrounded only by beautiful things, knowing that the drake he had captured would die in captivity. Note also the Lord's despising the disfigured chief steward (pages 7–8).

b. What do we learn about Shozo, the chief steward? Find the evidence to support your claim. Help students understand that Shozo is both obedient to his master, the lord of the district, but also compassionate about the captured drake.

c. Based on her actions of freeing the drake, what words might we use to describe Yasuko? How did the Lord of the district react? What were the consequences of Yasuko's actions?

Figure 4.8. Mandarin Duck Story Map

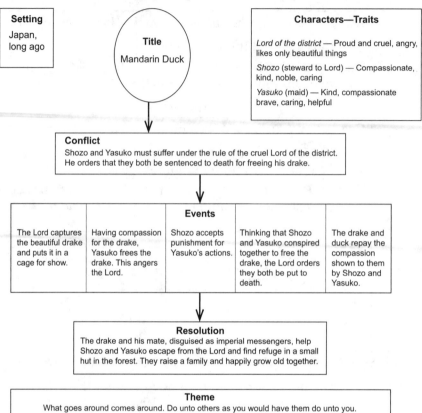

d. How do the traits of Shozo and Yasuko affect the outcome or ending of the story? What was the author inferring when she wrote that the drake and the duck "seemed to bow"? Help students understand that Shozo and Yasuko realize that the imperial messengers were really the drake and the duck in disguise who came back to help.

After Reading

1. Refer to the story map and review the characters and their traits as well as the events and outcome of the story.

2. Tell students that next they will see an animated film about the same story.
   Go to: http://video.nhptv.org/video/2238438897/

3. View the short 15-minute digital version of the story.

4. Next think about and make connections between the printed text and the digital version of the *Mandarin Ducks*.

Figure 4.9. *Mandarin Duck* and *Sweetest Fig* Template

<table>
<tr>
<td rowspan="2"></td>
<td colspan="2">Text 1: The Tale of the Mandarin Ducks (Paterson, 1990)
✓ Literary   ☐ Informational</td>
</tr>
<tr>
<td colspan="2">Text 2: The Sweetest Fig (Van Allsburg, 1993)
✓ Literary   ☐ Informational</td>
</tr>
<tr>
<td rowspan="3">Planning</td>
<td colspan="2">Grade-Level Standard (Lesson Objective):

RL4.9 Compare and contrast the treatment of similar themes and topics (e.g., opposition of good and evil) and patterns of events (e.g., the quest) in stories, myths, and traditional literature from different cultures.</td>
</tr>
<tr>
<td colspan="2">Writing Prompt Question: What are the themes of both stories, and how are they similar and different?</td>
</tr>
<tr>
<td colspan="2">Strategy: Use characters' traits and actions to determine the theme of a story.</td>
</tr>
<tr>
<td rowspan="3">Text Analysis</td>
<td>Similar Themes</td>
<td>Different Character Traits</td>
</tr>
<tr>
<td rowspan="2">Themes: The themes in both stories are about how a person's actions, whether good or bad, will often have similar consequences for that person.</td>
<td>Traits: Two characters who were compassionate: Shozo and Yasuko were kind, helpful, and compassionate toward other people and animals. They learned that their acts of kindness and helpfulness resulted in a life that ended in happiness.</td>
</tr>
<tr>
<td>Traits: Two characters who were cruel: Lord of the district and Monsieur Bibot were both cruel and unkind to people and animals. They cared more about themselves than others. They both learned that being mean, angry, and selfish resulted in a life of uncertainty.</td>
</tr>
<tr>
<td>Writing</td>
<td colspan="2">Text/Sentence Frame (scaffolded response to writing prompt):

The Tale of the Mandarin Ducks and The Sweetest Fig are similar and different in several ways. Two ways they are similar are the traits of the characters and the lessons they learned. For example, _____ and _____ were alike because _____. They both learned that _____. The characters _____ and _____ were also alike because they _____. However, they learned a different lesson. They learned that _____. The themes are also similar. In both stories, the themes are about _____.</td>
</tr>
</table>

5. Questions may include:

    a. How is the written text similar to the digital version?

    b. What are some differences between the printed text and the digital version?

    c. Does the printed text or the digital version give you a better sense of the story as a whole? What is it about the text or digital version that is better? What makes it better?

    d. What is one advantage of reading the book instead of seeing the digital version?

    e. What is one advantage of seeing the digital version instead of reading the book?

    f. What connections can you make between the book and the digital version?

    g. How does reading the book benefit you when you see the digital version?

    h. Would you rather see the digital version first or read the book? Why would you rather do that one first?

Writing Prompt:

What are the connections between the printed text and the digital version for The Tale of the Mandarin Ducks?

Support the students as they make connections between the book and the digital version about the Mandarin Ducks. Have them answer the prompt using the following story frame if they need this level of support.

Sentence Frame for *The Tale of the Mandarin Ducks*

Several connections can be made between the print text and the digital version of *The Tale of the Mandarin Ducks*. First, both the book and the digital version _____. Second, both the book and the digital version _____. However, there are also differences between the two texts. In the book, the illustrations show _____. In the digital version, the illustrations show _____. The _____ is better than the _____ because _____.

TEXT 2 (same as TEXT 1) Paterson, K. (1990). *The Tale of the Mandarin Ducks*. New York, NY: Scholastic.

1. Read the new objective for this set of lessons.

2. Explain that the theme of a story is the point or message of a story. Another way to think of the theme is the lesson that the main character learned by the end of the story. Explain that the author may not tell readers the theme, but that we, the readers, have to think about the characters and the events, or plot, to determine the theme-lesson or message of the story. Talk about lessons learned from familiar fairytales like *The Three Little Pigs* and *Goldilocks and the Three Bears*. Ask students what themes or lessons the pigs and Goldilocks may have learned from their experiences.

3. Reread and discuss *The Tale of the Mandarin Ducks*, referring to the important story elements recorded on the story map completed earlier (Figure 4.8). Use a story map to chart important story elements. Pay special attention to the thoughts and actions of the main characters that reveal each of their traits.

4. Ask students a different set of questions about the story.

    a. First, describe the traits of the Lord of the district. Do you think he lived to be old and happy? Why? What did the Lord of the district learn at the end of the story?

    b. How would you describe Shozo and Yasuko? What lesson do you think they learned? What can we learn from this, or, in other words, what is the theme of the story? Allow time for partners to share with each other. Help students understand that a person's actions, whether positive or negative, influence what happens to everyone. Refer to and discuss the theme of the story (Figure 4.8).

    TEXT 3   Van Allsburg, C. (1993). *The Sweetest Fig*. New York, NY: Houghton Mifflin Harcourt.

1. Tell students that they will read another story with a theme that is both similar and different from *The Tale of the Mandarin Ducks*.

2. Read and discuss *The Sweetest Fig*. Use a story map to chart important elements (Figure 4.10). Pay special attention to the thoughts and actions of the main characters that reveal each of their traits. Possible questions to ask:

    a. What do we know about Monsieur Bibot? What evidence from the story tells you about Monsieur Bibot's character? How do the illustrations help you understand Bibot's character? Find a good example to share with the class.

    b. How does Bibot feel about his dog, Marcel? Find evidence in the text to support your answer. (Draw particular attention to the strict and indifferent way that he treats Marcel throughout the story).

    c. What words could we use to describe Bibot, who would not give an old woman pain pills because she had no money?

Figure 4.10. *Sweetest Fig* **Story Map**

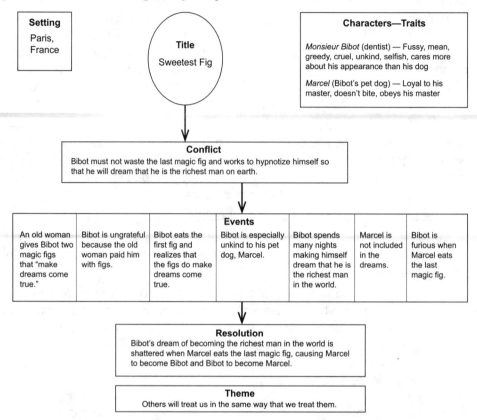

d. What words does the author use to let us know that the figs are really magic? What are Monsieur Bibot's plans? Locate the part that lets you know his plans. Where does Marcel fit into those plans?

e. How does the story change when Marcel eats the fig?

f. What does Marcel dream about? How do you know?

g. Based on what you have read so far, what do you think will happen next?

h. What did the author mean when he wrote that Bibot tried to yell, but all he could do was bark?

i. Did the figs really make dreams come true? If so, for whom and why?

After Reading

1. Determine the theme of the story. Ask:

   a. How did the lives of the characters change at the end of the story?

   b. What were the consequences of Monsieur Bibot's actions? What do you think he learned at the end of the story?

    c.   If he could talk, what do you suppose Marcel would tell us? Do you think that maybe Marcel learned a lesson as well? If so, what would that lesson be? Why?

    d.   Based on what both Monsieur Bibot and Marcel learned from this story, what message or theme did the author want readers to learn? Elicit from the students the concept that "what goes around, comes around"—or that a person's actions, whether good or bad, will often have consequences for that person.

Compare and Contrast Themes

Use a T-chart labeled SIMILAR and DIFFERENT. Tell the students that one way to compare and contrast the themes of the books is to look at both story maps (Figures 4.8 and 4.10) to determine what is similar and what is different. Help students understand that the themes in both stories are about how a person's actions, whether good or bad, will often have similar consequences for that person.

Writing Prompt

What are the themes of both stories, and how are they similar and different?

Sentence Frame for *Mandarin Ducks* and *Sweetest Fig*

Some students will benefit from the following paragraph frame to write a compare and contrast paragraph.

The Tale of the Mandarin Ducks and *The Sweetest Fig* are similar and different in several ways. Two ways they are similar are the traits of the characters and the lessons they learned. For example, _____ and _____ were alike because _____. They both learned that _____. The characters _____ and _____ were also alike because they _____. However, they learned a different lesson. They learned that _____. The themes are also similar. In both stories, the themes are _____.

STRATEGIC READING OF NARRATIVE TEXTS

The primary and intermediate set of lessons offered as models for reading across narrative texts are more effective and successful when supported with specific instruction in strategies that will help students better understand these texts. While many students can and do learn to read narratives on their own, it is useful to teach students specific strategies to use when reading multiple texts. After all, just because students understand a single narrative text does not mean they can transfer that knowledge when reading multiple texts. A situative theoretical perspective would suggest that students need plenty of practice to transfer the knowledge from a single text to multiple texts. These activities are different, so the learning will be different.

Story Map Strategies for Multiple Texts

As we know, the CCSS divides the standards for reading into three key dimensions: key ideas and details, authors' craft and structure, and integration of knowledge and ideas. There are all sorts of graphic organizers to help students recall and remember key ideas and details of narrative texts. The National Reading Panel (NICHD, 2000) found that graphic organizers like story maps help students' comprehension of the narratives they read. It is worthwhile to begin using the story map strategy in the 1st grade. It can be used in grades 2 and 3, with additional instruction in grades 4 and 5 as a starting-off point for deeper comprehension and analysis of individual and multiple texts.

The story map strategy involves developing a story line for each text that includes the key ideas and details of a text. Each day you can read a new book and then develop with students a story map for that book, as suggested in the lessons in this chapter. The story map helps students identify the main characters, setting, plot, main events, and resolution of a text they read. The map is important because it creates an internal mental template that students can use to monitor what is important and what to pay attention to in stories. The map also aids in selecting key details, remembering the text as a whole, and retrieving key ideas and details.

Side-by-side comparisons of the story maps help students see how the stories go together. This strategy is a beginning step toward helping students move to more complex analysis like compare and contrast. The visual picture serves as a reminder of the key idea and details of each story; the story map gives organization to each story.

Figure 4.11 shows the two story maps for the Three Bears and the Dinosaurs texts. The outlines serve as an important beginning to deeper analysis of the texts. Without an essential understanding of the key ideas and details, deeper analysis is not possible. Without story maps, young students who are asked to talk about how the Bears and Dinosaurs stories are alike and different are likely to pick out isolated parts of the stories. Using the story maps as an outline, students can more systematically determine similarities and differences. This leads to a deeper understanding of the texts.

One of this book's authors taught a lesson to 5th-graders on a story about a man and a boy in a middle of a river during a forest wildfire.

Figure 4.11. Side-by-Side Bears and Dinosaurs Story Maps

Text 1 (Three Bears)	Text 2 (Three Dinosaurs)
Setting: Bears' house	**Setting:** Dinosaurs' house
Characters: Goldilocks, Mama Bear, Papa Bear, Baby Bear	**Characters:** Goldilocks, Papa Dinosaur, Mama Dinosaur, Dinosaur from Norway
Problem: Goldilocks vandalizes Bears' house.	**Problem:** Dinosaurs set a trap to catch Goldilocks.
Events:	**Events:**
• Goldilocks enters bears' house and eats Baby Bear's porridge.	• Dinosaurs prepare chocolate pudding, then hide in the woods to wait for Goldilocks.
• She breaks Baby Bear's chair.	• Goldilocks barges into the Dinosaurs' house and eats all the pudding.
• She sleeps in Baby Bear's bed.	• She leaves the chairs alone—too tall for her.
• Bears return and find empty bowl and broken chair.	• She finds three big beds.
• Bears find Goldilocks sleeping in Baby Bear's bed.	• The dinosaurs yell they are going to "eat her up."
	• Goldilocks thinks, "This isn't the bears' house, it's the dinosaurs' house."
Resolution: Goldilocks is scared and runs away.	**Resolution:** Goldilocks knows she is going to be eaten up, so she runs away.

Her goal was a discussion and analysis of the boy's thoughtful reaction to a snake floating down the river and about to strike the man. The man could not see the snake, and the boy embarked on a lengthy discussion to keep the man calm. The problem with the lesson was that the 5th-graders did not understand the main problem of the story—that a snake was endangering the man's life, coiled up and ready to strike. The students thought the problem was the wildfire, not the snake. As a result, the students missed the main plot of the story. Using a story map and helping students through the plot of the story would have bridged this gap in knowledge for the students. After they understood the basic plot of the story, they could have then analyzed the character of the boy in more depth. As it was, however, students were not able to get to a deep level of understanding of the boy's character or the plot of the story.

Using Story Maps to Summarize Stories. Students can also use story maps to summarize the stories they read. This is an additional important use of a story map. Once students have identified and written down the appropriate characters, problem, and resolution, they can then pull out the sentences related to these three elements to make a short summary of what they read. Figure 4.12 shows how the character, problem, and resolution statements from Figure 4.11 can be used to summarize the two Goldilocks stories.

From the two summaries, teachers can ask students, "How are the stories alike and how are they different?" Their answers then will more likely focus on a deeper analysis of the difference in the two stories, that in one the Bears are harmless and Goldilocks is the vandal, and in the other, Goldilocks is harmless and the Dinosaurs are the bad guys. This is a critical difference that students may miss.

Answering Text-Dependent Questions

One important teaching strategy for reading narratives is to have students answer questions about what they read. This tried-and-true method has been in existence as long as teachers have taught, but research strongly supports its benefits (NICHD, 2000). However, the trick for teachers is to ask the appropriate questions for specific purposes. Not all questions are created equal. Improving comprehension with questions means developing a set of questions that leads students to deeper processing of text and deeper comprehension.

Webb's Depth of Knowledge Taxonomy. Developing a good set of questions for a text demands thought ahead of time. This is especially true with the new CCSS. The CCSS demands increasingly more complex questions moving toward literary analysis of narrative texts as students move up the grades. Many districts throughout the country now use Webb's Depth of Knowledge (DOK) Taxonomy of Questions (Webb, 2002) to help teachers develop thoughtful, text-dependent questions that require students to think deeply about what they read. Webb's taxonomy is similar to Bloom's taxonomy of questions (Krathwohl, 2002), except the DOK uses four levels of questions as opposed to the seven that Bloom uses.

The DOK uses active verbs to highlight the type of thinking required of students as they think about and analyze texts. Levels one and two

Figure 4.12. Story Map Elements for Story Summary

Goldilocks walks into the Bears' house and vandalizes the house. When the Bears return, she is scared and runs away.	The Dinosaurs set a trap to catch Goldilocks. She knows she is going to be eaten up so she runs away.

ask students basic questions about the text as well as some deeper questions that require students to infer, summarize, and interpret the texts, using verbs like "state," "recall," "recognize," "quote," and "report" at level one and "infer," "organize," "predict," "interpret," "compare," and "classify" at level two. Levels three and four ask students to think more deeply about text, using verbs like "assess," "revise," "formulate," "draw conclusions," "critique," and "investigate" at level three and "analyze," "prove," "create," and "synthesize" at level four.

The use of these different levels of the DOK and the verbs to go with them can help teachers develop effective questions that ask students to think deeply about the multiple literary texts they are reading. A circular chart on the web (Google: Webb's Depth of Knowledge) will assist teachers as they develop questions and activities that help students meet the standards in the CCSS.

Text-Dependent Questions. The CCSS also points to the importance of asking text-dependent questions. Text-dependent questions are those that can only be answered based on reading the text. For example, a text-dependent question for the two books *The Tale of the Mandarin Duck* and *The Sweetest Fig* might be:

"Examine the illustrations in both *The Tale of the Mandarin Duck* and *The Sweetest Fig*. How does each illustrator show readers the different emotions of the main characters? Which illustrator and author does a better job of showing those emotions? Provide evidence from the illustrations and the words in the texts to support your answer."

This is a text-dependent question because students must read and study both texts in order to be able to answer the question. Compare this question to the following one:

"In the books *The Tale of the Mandarin Duck* and *The Sweetest Fig*, both Bibot and the Lord of the district were mean and greedy men. Tell about someone you know who is mean and greedy."

This last comment/question is not text-dependent because students do not have to read either text to be able to respond. Students can answer just based on their background knowledge. In this case, students can exit the text itself to come up with an answer.

Current thinking based on CCSS standards encourages teachers to ask more text-dependent questions where students do not exit the text for an answer. Let's take another example. Which kind of question is this?

"Which of the characters in *Goldilocks and the Three Bears* and *Goldilocks and the Three Dinosaurs* do you like best?"

This is a personal-response question that asks students what they like. It does not force them to go back to the text for an answer. As such, it is not a text-dependent question. It could be modified, however, to formulate a text-dependent question by asking students to "Describe something that one of the characters did or said that made you like or dislike them."

The bulleted text-dependent questions in Figures 4.13 and 4.14 can help students think about and compare and contrast multiple texts. Teachers can choose which questions best fit the stories their students are reading. We have provided many different types of questions that focus on different elements of stories. The questions will vary with age and ability. Teachers will want to focus on a few questions for each set of texts they select.

When we look at the type of literary analysis that the CCSS demands, however, the text-dependent questions in Figures 4.13 and 4.14

Figure 4.13. Comparing and Contrasting Key Ideas and Details for Characters in Multiple Narrative Texts

- Identify the main characters of each story and tell how they are alike and different.
- What does each of the main characters want (what are the motives of each main character) and how are their goals similar and/or different?
- Who are other important characters in each story, and how do each of them compare and contrast with one another?
- How do the main characters interact with one another in each story? Do they interact with others in the same way or in a different way?
- How does each main character change over the course of the story?
- Tell the similarities and differences between the way the main characters change across stories.
- What are each main character's feelings and thoughts? How are they the same across stories, and how are they different?
- Quote from each text lines that show how each main character feels at first. Are these feelings the same or different and why?
- What challenges do the main characters face in each story? How are these challenges the same and/or different?
- Quote lines from each text that tell you how each main character reacts to their different situations. How would you compare and contrast these reactions?

Figure 4.14. Comparing and Contrasting Key Ideas and Details for Plots or Adventures in Multiple Narrative Texts

- State the main character's problem in each story and tell how they are the same or different.
- What is the major plot of each story? How do the plots differ or are they similar?
- Compare how each main character responds to the problem of each story.
- Compare and contrast the ways in which the plot is resolved in each story.
- Illustrate the way the plot was resolved in each story and compare the two resolutions.
- How do the main problems of the stories change over time? In what ways are these changes the same and/or different?
- How do the main characters each react to the problems in the story? In what ways are their reactions similar or different?
- State the main conflicts that occurred in each story and compare those conflicts.
- Describe the similarities and differences in the way the main characters reacted to the conflicts in the story.
- Compare and contrast how the conflicts were resolved in each story. How are they the same and different?

are not enough. They serve as a necessary, but not sufficient, starting point. Additional reading is required where students answer more complex questions in which they examine what the author does to create the characters, settings, events, and plots of the different narrative texts they read. Figure 4.15 presents a set of questions to compare and contrast different authors' craft and structure.

The CCSS asks students to go deeper into the text to talk about what the text means and to analyze it. Figures 4.16 and 4.17 focus on questions that will lead students to a deeper analysis of the text. Notice that these sets of questions focus on different elements of a narrative—the characters, setting, and so forth—and encourage students to read deeper into the text.

Providing Evidence

A way to strengthen the strategy of having students answer text-dependent questions is to have them find evidence in the text to support their answers. Providing evidence is a strategy all students must

Figure 4.15. Comparing and Contrasting Different Authors' Craft and Structure in Multiple Narrative Texts

- Identify the point of view each author writes from. Compare and contrast each author's point of view (first person, second person, third person).

- How do differences in point of view affect the stories authors tell and the readers who read them?

- Compare how each author engages the reader. What are the words and phrases each author uses? What are the strategies they use? How are they similar? How do the differences affect you as a reader?

a. For example, the author imagines a situation, uses the word "you," creates a dramatic situation, sets up a dilemma, begins with an anecdote.

- Do the authors use illustrations? What effect do the illustrations have on the reader? How do the illustrations compare and contrast with one another?

- What words and phrases let you know each author's tone? How are these the same or different?

- Compare and contrast each author's tone in the books. What do the words and phrases tell you?

- Where and why does each author use figurative language, similes, metaphors, and idiomatic expressions? How does the use of these words help the reader understand the story better?

- What are some words that each author uses to show you the motivations of the characters? How are the authors' words alike and different? Do the authors use similar or different strategies for showing you the motivation of the characters?

- What are some nuanced words that each author uses? How do these nuanced words help the reader understand the text better? How are these similar and different between the two (or more) authors?

- What are some words that elicit the reader's emotions in each piece? Are these emotions positive or negative? What adjectives does each author use to show emotions or feelings of characters? Are they similar or different?

be able to do to accomplish the many reading standards in the CCSS. It is also a critically important strategy to acquire in order to pass the new tests developed to measure the CCSS. In the future, most test questions will require students to find evidence directly from the text to support their responses.

Asking students to provide evidence from the text is a new and different activity for many of them. Often, in the course of student

Figure 4.16. Compare and Contrast the Knowledge and Ideas About the Characters in Multiple Narrative Texts

- Which character showed greater strength in the stories you read? How did that strength influence the outcome of the story?

- Compare and contrast the main characters' weaknesses. Is one weakness worse than another? In what ways? How do those weaknesses influence the outcomes of the stories?

- Analyze the way the two main characters responded to the major problem in each story. Compare the two responses. Which character responded in a better way? Why? How did that response influence the outcome of the story?

- Think about each main character. How did the authors let you know each of their thoughts and feelings? Compare and contrast each author's descriptions of the main characters. Which is more convincing to you? Why?

- Compare and contrast how each main character changed in the stories. What do those changes reveal about the main character?

Figure 4.17. Compare and Contrast Knowledge and Ideas About the Plots of Multiple Narrative Texts

- Compare and contrast the settings of the stories. How does each setting support the plot of each story?

- Compare and contrast the author's tone in the stories. How does each tone support the plot of each story?

- Compare and contrast the different plots of the stories. How does each plot support the theme of each story?

- How do the conflicts within each story move the plot of each story along?

- Think about how the events connect to one another and to the whole. Compare and contrast the stories and how the whole hangs together. Does one story do a better job at holding together than another? Why?

discussions in classrooms, a few students will automatically and effortlessly go back to the text to prove a point they want to make. But by and large, students will engage in discussions about a text without looking for support from the text itself. Struggling readers in particular do not know how to find a sentence or paragraph that contains the information they want. Often, for them the text is simply too difficult to navigate.

Scanning for Information. Struggling readers, as well as others who need support, can be helped by explicitly teaching them to scan for information using a scanning procedure where they look for keywords or phrases to focus on the part of the text that has the information they want. Figure 4.18 demonstrates how to teach students to scan for information. The point of scanning is that students do not have to go back and reread the whole text. All students should learn how to scan for information, especially as the CCSS tests will require students to provide evidence from the text.

Using Tools as Supports. Chapter 1 discussed the situative perspective and how conceptual tools help students learn more deeply. Both offline and online supports can provide students with a great deal of help and assistance. This is true for all learners, but especially true for underserved students, struggling readers, English language learners, and other students with special needs.

Offline supports for students as they navigate through multiple texts come in many forms. For example, sticky notes can come in handy for second and third reads of two texts to help students remember places where events, characters, and plots can be compared and contrasted. All students seem to enjoy using sticky notes. They encourage deep and active processing of texts. When students use sticky notes, they can highlight a particular area of text that will help them answer questions later on. They also write down their ideas, which then help them retain the information better. The more students write down their ideas, the better they learn. So using sticky notes can be a very effective way to scaffold finding evidence in texts to support answers to questions.

Similarly, highlighters and markers are also excellent tools for students to use to provide evidence in the texts they read. Narrow yellow highlighters are particularly useful for highlighting specific lines and words or phrases in texts. Markers can be used for the same purpose. Different-color markers can be used to compare different elements of two stories—green for comparing settings, red for comparing characters, yellow for comparing the authors' craft across multiple texts. Markers and highlighters can also be used for providing evidence to support an idea or an answer. Again, the value of these tools is that they encourage deep processing rather than superficial learning of the ideas in the text.

In addition to the many offline tools students can use to support their print reading, they can also use online tools for reading narrative texts. Online tools will help deepen comprehension of the multiple texts students read in important ways beyond what offline tools can do. Some of the online tools students and teachers can use include:

Figure 4.18. Scanning for Information

To scan for information, you move your eyes quickly down the page looking for specific words and phrases that are a part of the question and answer.

Follow these steps:

1. Read the selection.

2. Read each question completely.

3. Choose one or more keywords or important words from the question itself. Create an image of the keyword in your mind.

4. Use your pointer finger to move down the page until you find the word or phrase you want.

5. When your eye catches your keyword, read the surrounding sentences carefully to see if they help answer the question.

6. Reread the question to see if the information you found answers the question.

- videos and animation of many narrative texts
- audio support for the videos
- YouTube videos of the authors reading their own texts
- Internet articles about books, authors, and illustrators
- pictures and illustrations of books
- reviews of books

Consistent with a situative perspective of learning, these online supports all contribute to students' deeper understanding of the texts they read.

SUMMARY

> Narrative text is one type of literary text that describes the human experience. This type of text follows a predictable structure: characters, setting, and plot (problem/conflict, series of events, and solution/resolution).

> Students' awareness of story structure facilitates their comprehension of narratives. As students progress through the grades, they will encounter more complex texts with more sophisticated story structures.

> Vocabulary in narrative texts tends to contain a higher percentage of rare words than informational texts. Authors rely on nuances of word meanings to precisely convey story elements, often using many and varied words that may be unfamiliar to students.

➢ With the increased demands of students integrating and comparing/ contrasting information across complex texts, teachers can scaffold the instruction for students by incorporating a variety of strategies. These include the use of graphic organizers such as story maps, asking text-dependent questions, supporting answers with evidence from the text, and scanning for information.

CHAPTER 5

Reading and Understanding Informational Texts

The move from narrative to informational texts represents a step up in difficulty because, as Graesser and his colleagues (1991) pointed out, informational texts are harder to read and understand. Despite the increased difficulty, most students enjoy informational texts a great deal; many even prefer them (Mohr, 2003; Wolfersberger, Reutzel, Sudweeks, & Fawson, 2004).

This chapter begins with a story from Ms. Steenson's 1st-grade class, a class that loved studying about ants. Ms. Steenson read several books about ants, including *Kids Ants* (Stewart, 2010), *The Life and Times of the Ant* (Micucci, 2006), and *Ant Cities* (Scott Foresman, 1990). Based on their readings, her students learned all about ants and wrote about what they learned. Some of the texts used vocabulary that young 1st-graders might find difficult. For example, "dynasty," "ramble," "solitary," "survive," and "pheromones" are all unique words found in the beginning pages of *The Life and Times of the Ant*. Nevertheless, because students were engaged in a topic of ants and because they were provided with the appropriate amount of support, these informational texts opened new worlds for Ms. Steenson's students.

Most students can handle informational texts with help. There are two important points to note here about reading informational texts. First, students will often need help with content that may be unfamiliar to most of them. In Ms. Steenson's class, for example, her students knew very little about ants and ant colonies. Second, most students will need help with the structure of informational texts because that is also unfamiliar to them. Most students in Ms. Steenson's class had not been introduced to informational texts. Yet, with encouragement, discussion, and support, students can learn a great deal about how informational texts work and how they deliver knowledge, concepts, and ideas to their readers. While most of the information was new to Ms. Steenson's students, the unifying topic—ants—was not. These insects are known and interesting to most children. With support, Ms. Steenson's students loved learning more about ants and grew very knowledgeable about them (Figures 5.1 and 5.2).

Figure 5.1. Ant Colonies

Figure 5.2. Informational Text on Ants

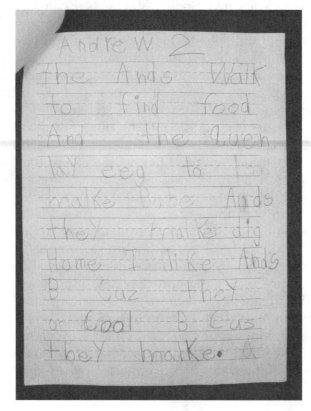

This chapter follows the same organization as Chapter 4, beginning with a discussion of the specific challenges of informational texts, followed by primary- and intermediate-grade examples of lessons to guide instruction for Standards 7 and 9 for Informational Texts (Figure 5.3). Finally, strategies are offered that support teachers and students to improve reading across multiple informational texts.

WHY ARE INFORMATIONAL TEXTS SO IMPORTANT?

Generally speaking, we all need to learn how to read various informational materials for one purpose or another. In schools and universities, students are expected to understand and learn bodies of knowledge from health, history, civics, geography, and science textbooks. In the workplace, adults are expected to read numerous informational materials to be informed, for example, about a potentially beneficial medicine, about a new procedure, about a change in schedules. In society, adults are expected to be able to read and understand all kinds of informational text—from printed tickets to job applications to newspapers and magazines.

Informational materials have been shown to be more difficult to read than narrative materials (Graesser et al., 1991). In studies done with adult readers, researchers have found that readers take longer to read informational materials than narrative materials. In addition, readers are less likely to understand and remember what they read when they read informational texts than when they read narratives.

By the time students reach the intermediate grades, they usually have had considerable experience and instruction in reading literature, for example, short stories, novels, fairytales, myths, legends, and poems. However, they have far less experience and instruction in reading informational texts, for example, content-area textbooks, newspapers, magazines, brochures, essays, editorials, persuasive pieces, directions and instructions, and airline and bus schedules. Duke's now-classic study (2000) revealed that the 1st-graders she observed spent 3.6 minutes a day on informational texts. While this amount of time has likely improved over the last decade, students still don't have enough experiences with informational texts. That is certainly one of the reasons the CCSS focuses attention on informational texts.

Figure 5.3. Anchor Standards 7 and 9

Anchor Standard 7 for Informational Texts: Integrate and evaluate content presented in diverse media and formats, including visually and quantitatively, as well as in words.

Anchor Standard 9 for Informational Texts: Compare and contrast the major points and key details in two texts on the same topic.

Unfamiliar Content and Vocabulary

One reason why informational materials are harder to read than narrative materials is that informational texts often contain content that is unfamiliar. As a matter of fact, this is one reason we pick up informational materials—we want to learn from them. We read a text for a class so that we will learn more. We read a bus schedule to know what time our bus arrives. We read a newspaper to learn the news of the day.

A second but related reason why informational materials are harder to read and understand is that these texts often contain new vocabulary representing new concepts. Consider Seymour Simon's book *Weather* (2006). The text uses specific science vocabulary and concepts that are difficult to follow if unfamiliar. To understand the text, readers need some background knowledge about *cumulus clouds* and also about the concept of "strongly rising air currents" preceding a cold front. They also need some conception of how high these *cumulonimbus clouds* go and of how high the *troposphere* is. They would be helped by knowledge about the weather/rain cycle as well. Some of the vocabulary is illustrated in the text, but without additional knowledge of several other vocabulary words and concepts, readers have a hard time understanding the text.

Vocabulary is certainly one area that makes reading informational texts more difficult than narratives. As we discussed in the last chapter, in narrative texts authors use many different words to mean the same thing; for example, *walking* can become *traipsing, barging, sauntering, strolling,* and *meandering.* Even though these words have nuanced meanings, they still generally refer to some type of walking. And, generally, students have a conception of the concept. Even though they may not know what traipsing means, they know what walking means. In informational texts, however, different words mean concepts that have very specific and denotational meanings. For example, writers cannot substitute *cumulous clouds* for *cirrus clouds* or *stratus clouds.* Each type of cloud is one particular kind, and one type cannot be substituted for another. Further, generally students often do not have existing conceptions of the words' meanings.

This is a critical point that Hiebert makes (Hiebert, 2010, 2012, 2013), and it is one of the most important aspects of informational texts that contribute to their difficulty. In informational texts, particularly in the disciplines of science, social studies, and math, writers use very specific vocabulary terms that often represent important conceptual distinctions. These words cannot be substituted for one another, and there are no nuanced meanings that can substitute. Therefore, if students do not know the concepts, comprehension will be impaired.

Thus, texts become harder with the use of many new and unfamiliar concepts. But context is important, too. More new words can be presented if there is a rich context that helps students figure out the meanings of the new words. For example, in the Simon text, the different types of clouds are illustrated with pictures of each type —cumulus, cirrus, and stratus—and a chart shows the path of a cold front arising from air currents. In this case the *Weather* text becomes easier to read and understand.

Thus, vocabulary is often part of the body of knowledge needed to comprehend a given informational text. The more unfamiliar the content of a given text is, including the vocabulary, the harder that text is to read and understand. Because informational materials often contain new content as well as new vocabulary terms, readers often have a harder time understanding them than they do the literary texts they read.

Unfamiliar Structure

Another source of difficulty for informational texts is that they often contain different text structures within the same text. Chapter 4 showed how narratives have one essential text structure, the story structure. Although there are variations of a story structure, and although they become more complex as students get older, the narrative story structure remains fairly consistent across most narrative texts.

On the other hand, researchers have identified several different text structures in informational texts. Armbruster and Anderson (1984) and Meyer (1975) identified several: question/answer, description, sequence, cause/effect, problem/solution, and compare/contrast.

These different structures cause problems for readers for a number of reasons.

- A number of different text structures can appear in a long passage, article, or book.
- Readers are often unaware of the different structures.
- Writers sometimes do not cue readers into the structure by using signal or cue words—*but, because, on the one hand, in comparison,* and so forth.
- Teachers do not often teach students to be aware of these different text structures.
- Readers can get buried in the new vocabulary and concepts and not look for the overarching organization of the text.

Using Text Structure to Understand Informational Texts

The main reason why text structures are important is that they help readers organize the information in the text so that readers can more easily identify the key ideas and details of the texts they read. Indeed, a text's structure is often the key to summarizing the text. For example, in *Volcano* (Lauber, 1986), the text's overall structure is cause and effect. Lauber shows through pictures, charts, and text the devastating results of Mount St. Helens after it erupted. Being able to identify that overall structure helps students summarize the text, since a summary can come from the identification of the cause (the volcano erupting) and the effect (the various details about what happened as a result of the erupting volcano). This summary can then be used to synthesize information across multiple texts.

Without an understanding of the overall structure of a text, students' thinking often jumps around with fragmented details instead of focusing on the key ideas. When writing summaries, many students, especially lower-achieving readers, struggle to figure out the main points of a text and to summarize it. They retreat to a recall of all the information they can remember or a random assortment of bits of information. They may have little idea of what is important and what is not. So they go through a text in a piece-by-piece manner, often moving from one small detail to the next. They do not sense the overall organization of the text or passages within it. As a result, their key ideas and details are often not those that the author considers relevant.

Once students can identify the structure of a text, they can then identify the main points and the details that support those points. From there, it is relatively easy to summarize a text.

The following section shows a set of primary and intermediate lessons using informational texts.

PRIMARY-GRADE INFORMATIONAL EXAMPLE

This first example focuses on a kindergarten and first-grade set of lessons on butterflies (Figure 5.4). This example combines informational text with digital text to allow students to learn about butterflies and to compare and contrast information and illustrations in four different texts.

Figure 5.4. *Butterflies* Template

	Text 1: Butterflies (Neye, 2000)
	☐ Literary ✓ Informational (digital version)
	Text 2: Beautiful Butterflies (Goldish, 2008)
	☐ Literary ✓ Informational
	Text 3: Monarch Butterfly: Caterpillar and Butterfly Facts for Kids (Louis, 2013)
	☐ Literary ✓ Informational (digital text)
	Text 4: From Caterpillar to Butterfly (Heiligman, 1996)
	☐ Literary ✓ Informational

Figure 5.4. *Butterflies* Template (continued)

Planning	***Grade-Level Standard*** (Lesson Objectives): **RI1.7.** Use the illustrations and details in a text to describe its key ideas. **RI1.9**. Identify basic similarities in and differences between two texts on the same topic (e.g., in illustrations, descriptions, or procedures).
	Writing Prompt Question: How is the information in different books about butterflies the same or different?
	Strategy: Compare and contrast information using text and text features.

Text Analysis	**Text 1: *Butterflies***	**Text 2: *Beautiful Butterflies***
	• Live all over world • Insects • Six legs and wings • Different sizes and colors • Egg → caterpillar → hard shell → adult • Use tongue to suck juices from flowers • Some sleep in winter, others fly south PICTURES • Illustrations	• Insects with large wings • Different sizes and colors • Six legs and antennas • Use front feet to taste food • Use beak to suck nectar from flowers • Egg → caterpillar → chrysalis →adult • Fly to warm places in winter PICTURES • Photographs • Captions (inside leaves) • Labels
	Text 3: *Monarch Butterfly*	**Text 4: *From Caterpillar to Butterfly***
	• Starts as an egg • Caterpillar eats for days • Monarch butterflies eat milkweed plants • Chrysalis • Adult PICTURES • Photographs • Captions	• Starts as an egg • Caterpillar eats and eats and eats • Chrysalis • Adult PICTURES • Illustrations • Captions

Writing	***Text/Sentence Frame*** (scaffolded response to writing prompt): We read four books about butterflies. In these books we learned that _____. However, the books were different because _____.

LESSON—BUTTERFLIES

Grades K–1

TEXT 1   Neye, E. (2000). *Butterflies*. New York, NY: Penguin Young Readers.

1. Read the objectives with students. Tell the students that they are going to learn about butterflies by reading four different texts. They will also compare and contrast the information in these four books. In other words, they will tell how the information presented in the books is the same and how it is different. One way to do this is to compare what is written in each text. Another way is to look at the pictures and see how they are the same and different.

    a. Use examples to introduce the difference between an illustration and a photograph. Help students understand that an illustration is not a picture of a real butterfly. Someone drew it and used different colors to make the image look like a butterfly. The person who drew the illustrations is called an illustrator. A photograph is more real-looking. Someone used a camera to take the picture. This person is called a photographer.

2. Read and discuss *Butterflies*. Chart information about butterflies (refer to Figure 5.4) as well as attributes of the pictures. Draw students' attention to how the author used the illustrations to support and extend information in the text. Possible questions to ask:

    a. What do we know about butterflies from reading these pages?

    b. What information about butterflies did we learn from the illustrations?

    c. How do the illustrations help us better understand what we just read?

After Reading

1. Use the illustrations to review information about butterflies. Select illustrations that draw students' attention to major concepts (e.g., butterflies live everywhere, butterflies are insects, butterflies come in different sizes and colors, and butterflies have a specific life cycle).

Writing

    a. Explain to students that they will now have a chance to be an author and illustrator by creating their own books about butterflies (Figure 5.5).

    b. Have students write their names on the cover page of the book. Then instruct students to create page 1 of their books by drawing a picture of something they learned today about butterflies.

Figure 5.5. My Butterfly Book

My Butterfly Book

Written and illustrated by _____

_____

_____

PARTS OF A BUTTERFLY

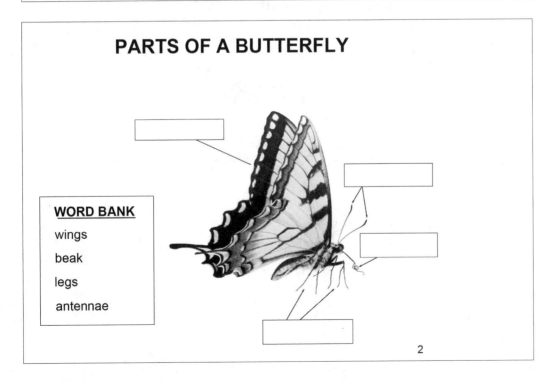

WORD BANK

wings

beak

legs

antennae

2

Figure 5.5. My Butterfly Book (continued)

On this page the teacher places a photograph of a butterfly taken from the Internet, magazine article, or book.

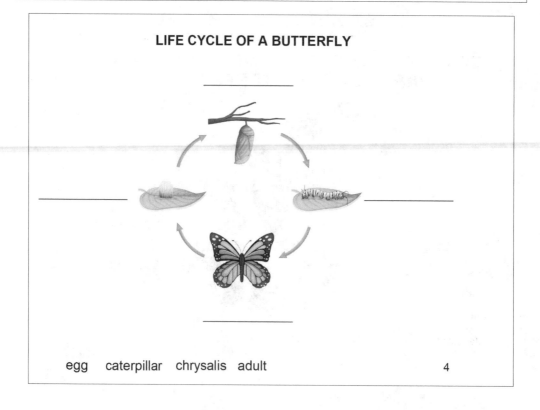

LIFE CYCLE OF A BUTTERFLY

egg   caterpillar   chrysalis   adult   4

TEXT 2   Goldish, M. (2008). *Beautiful Butterflies*. New York, NY: Bearport Publishing.

1. Tell students that they will read another book about butterflies and that they will compare and contrast it with the book they read in the previous lesson.

2. Introduce *Beautiful Butterflies*. Draw students' attention to the photographs in the book. Ask how these are the same and different than the illustrations in the book read yesterday.

3. Read *Beautiful Butterflies*. Chart information about butterflies (Figure 5.4) and what the photographs show as well.

   a. Ask students if the information they are learning is similar to or different from the information listed on the chart created for the book read yesterday. Place a check (✓) beside similar information found in both books.

   b. Point out the captions, such as the one on page 4. Explain that authors use captions to give more information about the pictures on the page.

   c. Point out the labels and their purpose, such as the one on page 7. Explain that labels usually have lines or arrows pointing to something. Captions do not.

After Reading

1. Use the chart to compare and contrast texts.

   a. Review the information about butterflies. Ask students to identify the information that they found in both books (checked items). Then have students turn to a partner and tell something that was mentioned in both books. Have them begin their sentence with, "In both books we learned that _____."

   b. Ask the students how the books are different. Draw their attention to those items that do not have checks next to them as well as differences in the pictures. Have students explain something different in both books to a partner using the following sentence frame: "The books are different because _____."

   c. You may choose to have students complete the following paragraphs:

   We read two books about butterflies. In both books we learned that _____.

   However, the books were different because _____.

Extension

Distribute students' copies of "My Butterfly Book." Reinforce the use of labels by having students fill in the boxes that correctly identify the parts of the butterfly on page 2 (Figure 5.5).

TEXT 3   Louis, M. (2013). *Monarch Butterfly: Caterpillar and Butterfly Facts for Kids*. [Kindle version]. Available at Amazon.com

1. Tell the students that they are going to compare and contrast two more books about butterflies. Explain that both of these books focus on how butterflies grow from tiny eggs into beautiful butterflies.
2. Read and discuss *Monarch Butterfly: Caterpillar and Butterfly Facts for Kids*. Explain that this book is not printed on paper. Rather, this book is "digital" because it must be downloaded and read from a tablet or computer. Chart information about butterflies from the text and photographs.

After Reading

1. Use the chart (Figure 5.4) to review stages of the monarch butterfly.
2. Distribute students' copies of "My Butterfly Book." Provide students with a picture of a butterfly to glue on page 3 of their books. Have students glue the picture of the butterfly on page 3 of their books. Instruct students to write a caption for their photograph. Ask students to use labels as well to point out features and elements found in the photograph that enhance understanding of the life cycle of the butterfly.

TEXT 4   Heiligman, D. (1996). *From Caterpillar to Butterfly*. New York, NY: HarperCollins.

1. Review the objectives.
2. Follow the same procedure to read and chart information (Figure 5.4) in *From Caterpillar to Butterfly*. Make sure to check information that is the same in this text and the previously read texts.

After Reading

1. Follow the same procedure used with the first two books for comparing and contrasting texts (Figure 5.4):
    a. Ask students to identify information about the stages of the butterfly that was the same in texts 3 and 4 (checked items). Then have students turn to a partner and tell something that was mentioned in both texts. Have them

begin their sentence with, "In both texts about the stages of butterflies we learned that _____."

b. Ask the students how the books are different. Draw their attention to those items that do not have checks next to them as well as differences in the pictures. Have students explain something different in both books to a partner using the following sentence frame: "The books are different because _____."

Writing Prompt

How is the information in different books about butterflies the same or different?

Students can use the sentence frame below if they need help writing about how butterfly books are the same and different.

We read two books about stages of butterflies. In both books we learned that _____. However, the books were different because _____.

Butterflies Extension

Have students complete page 4 of their butterfly books by writing about the different stages of the life cycle of a butterfly.

Additional Multimedia Resources

In addition to texts on butterflies, there are numerous online resources that teachers and students may find useful as they explore this topic. These include:

- The Children's Butterfly Site: http://www.kidsbutterfly.org
- National Geographic Kids: http://kids.nationalgeographic.com/kids/animals/creaturefeature/monarch-butterflies/
- National Geographic Butterfly Videos: http://video.nationalgeographic.com/video/kids/animals-pets-kids/bugs-kids/butterflies-kids/
- Migration of Monarch Butterflies: http://video.nationalgeographic.com/video/kids/animals-pets-kids/bugs-kids/monarch-butterflies-kids
- San Diego Zoo: http://kids.sandiegozoo.org/animals/insects/butterfly

INTERMEDIATE-GRADE INFORMATIONAL EXAMPLE

The next set of lessons revolves around the ever-fascinating sinking of the *Titanic* (Figure 5.6). In these lessons many different genres of

Figure 5.6. *Titanic* Template

<table>
<tr><td rowspan="3"></td><td colspan="2">Text 1: TITANIC Disaster at Sea (Jenkins & Sanders, 2008)
☐ Literary ✓ Informational</td></tr>
<tr><td colspan="2">Text 2: The Sinking of the Titanic: Excerpts from an Eyewitness Account (http://altnersandi.com/2012/03/25/titanic-survivor-esther-bloomfield-hart-recalls-tragic-sinking/)
☐ Literary ✓ Informational</td></tr>
<tr><td colspan="2">Text 3: Titanic Survivor Esther Bloomfield Hart Recalls Tragic Sinking (http://www.newsbankschools.com/schools/pdf/SinkingOfTheTitanic.pdf)
☐ Literary ✓ Informational</td></tr>
<tr><td rowspan="3">Planning</td><td colspan="2">Grade-Level Standard (Lesson Objective):
RI4.7. Interpret information presented visually, orally, or quantitatively (e.g., in charts, graphs, diagrams, time lines, animations, or interactive elements on Web pages) and explain how the information contributes to an understanding of the text in which it appears.
RI5.9. Integrate information from several texts on the same topic in order to write or speak about the subject knowledgeably.</td></tr>
<tr><td colspan="2">Writing Prompt Question: How are the firsthand accounts of two survivors of the Titanic similar and different, and what new insights do we learn from them?</td></tr>
<tr><td colspan="2">Strategy: Students compare and contrast multiple points of view.</td></tr>
<tr><td rowspan="2">Text Analysis</td><td>Similar</td><td>Different</td></tr>
<tr><td>EVENTS
• Both bravely survived the sinking of the Titanic
• Both witness Titanic front “dive” into ocean
• Both lose family/friends
• Both rescued by Carpathia
FEELINGS
• Both deeply affected by the traumatic events
• Feeling of helplessness</td><td>EVENTS
• E.H.-passenger; H.B.-crew
• E.H.-dreaded being on ship; H.B.-experienced at sailing
• E.H. hears ship hitting iceberg; H.B. did not hear collision
• E.H.-allowed onto lifeboat; H.B. washed into ocean and climbed aboard upturned lifeboat
• H. B. severely injured
FEELINGS
• E.H.-frantic from onset; H.B. not concerned at first—even joked</td></tr>
</table>

Figure 5.6. *Titanic* Template (continued)

Writing	*Text/Sentence Frame* (scaffolded response to writing prompt):
	Esther Hart and Harold Bride both survived the sinking of the Titanic. Their experiences were similar in some ways. According to Esther Hart, "_____." According to Harold Bride, "_____." Even though they lived through the same event, their experiences were also different. For example, Esther Hart _____. She said, "_____." She also _____. She also said, "_____." On the other hand, Harold Bride _____. He said, "_____." He also _____. He said, "_____."

informational texts—from eyewitness accounts in dairies to printed texts to newspaper articles available on the Internet—can be used to help intermediate-grade students build a deeper understanding of the events that dramatically played out on a ship in the middle of the Atlantic Ocean in 1912.

LESSON—*TITANIC SURVIVORS*

Grades 4–5

TEXT 1   Jenkins, M., & Sanders, B. (2008). *TITANIC Disaster at Sea.* Somerville, MA: Candlewick Press.

1. Read the objectives with students. Tell these students that the purpose of the following lessons is to compare and contrast the personal accounts of two survivors of the *Titanic* disaster. In order to do this, they will first read a book to build background knowledge about the people and events associated with this tragedy.

2. Build background of the event by reading, discussing, and charting portions of *TITANIC Disaster at Sea.* Use the following questions to focus on those pages that deal with the experiences of those on board the ship:

    a. What was the role of the Marconi operators (wireless radio technology)? How was this "standard" form of communication of 1912 different from the technology available today? What impact did the actions of the Marconi operators have on the outcome of the disaster (pages 8, 14–15)? What choices did other crew members make and how did their choices impact the event?

    b. Describe various reasons passengers had for sailing on the *Titanic*. How did the accommodations differ for first-, second-, and third-class passengers (pages 8, 14–15)? What factors influenced a person's chance of survival, e.g. male, female, children, adults, first-, second- or third-class, crew member versus passengers (analyze the chart on page 30)?

c.   What took place during the final hours (pages 22–28)?

d.   As a consequence of the *Titanic* tragedy, what modifications were made to make travel safer?

Writing

After reading and discussing the text, have students work in small groups or with a partner to create a timeline that describes the events that occurred during the final hours of the tragedy.

TEXT 2   "Titanic Survivor Esther Bloomfield Hart Recalls Tragic Sinking" (http://altnersandi.com/2012/03/25/titanic-survivor-esther-bloomfield-hart-recalls-tragic-sinking/)

1.   Read the objectives again with students. Tell them that the next account they will read is about a second-class passenger on the *Titanic*, Esther Hart. Explain that because she is describing her experiences in her own words, this account is being told in first person. Note and discuss the difference between this text and Text 1, written in the third person. Also note that this text is digital and not in print. Remind students that they can learn much about an event or topic from reading online as well as from texts.

2.   Read and discuss the text. Use a chart to note the events and personal feelings of her experience (Figure 5.6). Possible questions to ask:

a.   What was Esther's purpose for sailing on the *Titanic*? How did she feel about making the voyage?

b.   Describe the events that led to her ending up in a lifeboat and being rescued. Why did she get a spot on the boat and not others? What words did she use to explain her feelings?

c.   How did Esther's life change as a result of being a survivor? What hardships did she face? Explain.

d.   How did the use of first-person point-of-view influence your understanding of and feelings about this event as opposed to the third-person point-of-view used in *TITANIC Disaster at Sea*?

After Reading

1.   Using the chart (Figure 5.6) have students work with a partner or in small groups to write a summary of the events that happened and Esther's feelings about those events.

2. Ask students to describe the difference between reading this personal account and the first text's description of events and people.

3. As an extension, have students listen to and discuss the interview with Eva Hart, the daughter of Esther Hart, who was also a survivor: http://www.bbc.co.uk/archive/titanic/5058.shtml

> TEXT 3   "The Sinking of the Titanic: Excerpts from an Eyewitness Account" http://www.newsbankschools.com/schools/pdf/SinkingOfTheTitanic.pdf
>
> Actual article: http://query.nytimes.com/mem/archive-free/pdf?res=F10D11FE3E5813738DDDA00994DC405B828DF1D3
> Condensed version: http://www.encyclopedia-titanica.org/titanic-survivor/harold-sydney-bride.html

1. Review the objectives. Tell students that they will read an account by another survivor who was a Marconi operator on the ship. As they read, have them think of how the experiences of these two people were similar and different.

2. Use the same format to read and chart information as with Esther Hart's account (Figure 5.6). Possible similar questions to ask:

   a. What was Harold's role on the *Titanic*? How did he feel about his job on the *Titanic*?

   b. Describe the events that led to his ending up in a lifeboat and being rescued. Why did he get a spot on the boat and not others? What words did he use to explain his feelings?

   c. How did his life change as a result of being a survivor? Explain.

After Reading

1. Using the chart (Figure 5.6) have the students talk with a partner to summarize the events as described by Harold.

2. Ask students to describe the differences between reading Harold's personal account and the first text's description of events and people.

3. As an extension, have students view a video that depicts Harold's experience: http://www.youtube.com/watch?v=SUshzSTkJpA

Comprehension Strategy Instruction: Compare and Contrast Experiences

Place the charts of both personal accounts side-by-side (Figure 5.6) and review the experiences of Esther and Harold. Have students look through both lists for similarities and differences. Help students understand that although both people survived the same event, their experiences were still different. Chart students' responses.

Writing Prompt

How are the firsthand accounts of two survivors of the Titanic similar and different, and what new insights do we learn from them?

Have students use the chart to talk to a partner about similarities and differences of both accounts. Have students write a compare/contrast paragraph. Some students may benefit from the following paragraph frame to write a compare-and-contrast paragraph.

Sentence Frame for Accounts of the *Titanic*

Esther Hart and Harold Bride both survived the sinking of the *Titanic*. Their experiences were similar in some ways. According to Esther Hart, "_____." According to Harold Bride, "_____." Even though they lived through the same event, their experiences were also different. For example, Esther Hart _____. She said, "_____." She also _____. She also said, "_____." On the other hand, Harold Bride _____. He said, "_____." He also _____. He said, "_____."

Esther Hart Accounts

http://altnersandi.com/2012/03/25/titanic-survivor-esther-bloomfield-hart-recalls-tragic-sinking/

Interview with Esther Hart's daughter, Eva Hart, http://www.bbc.co.uk/archive/titanic/5058.shtml

Harold Bride Accounts

The Sinking of the *Titanic*: Excerpts from an Eyewitness Account, http://www.newsbankschools.com/schools/pdf/SinkingOfTheTitanic.pdf

Actual article: http://query.nytimes.com/mem/archive-free/pdf?res=F10D11FE3E5813738DDDA00994DC405B828DF1D3

Harold Bride and Pictures

http://www.encyclopedia-titanica.org/titanic-survivor/harold-sydney-bride.html

http://forgottennewsmakers.com/2010/07/19/harold-bride-1890-%E2%80%93-1956-wireless-operator-on-the-titanic/

http://www.youtube.com/watch?v=SUshzSTkJpA

Account of Another Survivor, Elizabeth Shutes

The Sinking of the *Titanic*, 1912, http://www.eyewitnesstohistory.com/titanic.htm

Additional Books and Multimedia Resources

- Learning about the *Titanic* and its fateful demise can be a fascinating topic for students of all ages. The following books and websites provide a wide variety of resources to support in-depth study about the ship, its crew and passengers, and the events leading up to and following the disaster:

Books

- Brewster, H., & Coulter, L. (1998). *882 ½ Amazing Answers to your Questions about the Titanic.* New York, NY: Scholastic.
- Carson, M. K. (2012). *Good Question: What Sank the World's Biggest Ship and Other Questions about the Titanic.* New York, NY: Sterling Children's Books.
- Korman, G. (2011). *Titanic, Book One: Unsinkable.* New York, NY: Scholastic.
- Korman, G. (2011). *Titanic, Book Two: Collision Course.* New York, NY: Scholastic.
- Korman, G. (2011). *Titanic, Book Three: S.O.S.* New York, NY: Scholastic.
- Stewart, D., & Antram, D. (2013). *You Wouldn't Want to Sail on the Titanic.* New York, NY: Scholastic.

Websites

- www.encyclopedia-titanica.org

This extensive website includes passenger and crew biographies, information about the ship, pictures, articles, and ongoing discussions about the disaster.

- http://www.nmni.com/titanic

The National Museums Northern Ireland Titanic Website offers information about the design and construction of the ship as well as personal stories, photographs, and videos.

- www.titanicphotographs.com

This is the picture library of Father Browne, who was a first-class passenger on the *Titanic*. This picture library is one of the most important collections of images from the *Titanic's* maiden voyage.

- www.nationalarchives.gov.uk/titanic/

The National Archives (UK) informational website includes a selection of images as well as a timeline, passenger stories, videos, podcasts, and other educational resources.

- www.rmstitanic.net

RMS Titanic, Inc. recovered over 5,500 artifacts during research expeditions. You can explore the wreck site through interactive photos and videos available in the Expedition Titanic section.

- www.immersionlearning.org

Immersion Learning is a nonprofit science education organization that provides a "Return to the Titanic" online page and *Titanic*-themed games.

- http://www.pbs.org/lostliners/

The PBS Lost Liners website includes information about five lost liner archaeological expeditions: *Lusitania, Titanic, Empress of Ireland, Britannic,* and *Andrea Doria.*

Interactive Websites and Games about the Titanic:

- Mapping Shipwrecks!—Immersion Learning

Students can arrange images to make a photomosaic of a shipwreck, then zoom in to explore the wreck. One of the shipwrecks featured is RMS Titanic.

- www.jason.org/immersion-learning/games
- Titanic Moviemaker—Immersion Learning http://www.immersionlearning.org/

Students can combine video clips of *Titanic* and the wreck to create their own *Titanic* movie.

- www.teachertube.com/viewVideo.php?video_id=228583
- Adventure on the Titanic—Interactive Game—National Geographic

This is a strategic online game that allows you to travel aboard the *Titanic* as a first-class passenger and complete quest cards while you explore the decks. Clicking on the "White Star" flag emblems during the game allows you to learn more about actual people and places on the *Titanic.*

- www.channel.nationalgeographic.com
- On Board The Titanic—Discovery.com

Macromedia Flash movies allows students to follow the paths of actual Titanic passengers.

- www.news.discovery.com/history/tags/titanic.htm
- Titanic Interactive—History.com

This interactive site provides exploration of the *Titanic* to learn about its construction, its ill-fated maiden voyage, and the survivors who lived to tell their stories.

- www.history.com/interactives/titanic-interactive
- A Titanic Timeline, 1909–2012 [Interactive]—Scientific American

An interactive timeline showing key moments in *Titanic* history.

- www.scientificamerican.com
- Morse Code Translator

Students can type in a message and listen to it play in Morse code.

- www.morsecode.scphillips.com/jtranslator.html

STRATEGIC READING OF MULTIPLE INFORMATIONAL TEXTS

In order for students to learn to read and write about multiple texts, they need learning strategies to help them. Many learning strategies are particularly effective for reading informational text. One of the most important points here is that we want students to use multiple texts to deepen their learning. This requires not only the reading of texts, but also the viewing of digital information, including graphs, charts, diagrams, illustrations, and so forth.

Using Graphic Organizers

One important way to compare and contrast informational texts is through the use of graphic organizers. There are several different types of graphic organizers students can use to organize and summarize information from individual texts. By using graphic organizers, students can more easily figure out the important information in a text than they can without one. They also can more easily summarize a text. They can then use the graphic organizers and/or summaries to compare and contrast two or more texts.

Here we show you different kinds of graphic organizers to go with the different structures of informational texts. It is important to make sure that the graphic organizer you select goes with the structure of the text. In other words, you can't use just any graphic organizer with any text. The structure of the text must fit the graphic organizer.

Question/Answer Graphic Organizers. To help students understand and use information in a question/answer structure, students can use the Question/Answer Graphic Organizer. We demonstrate the use of this kind of organizer through questions and answers from different texts about the _Titanic_ (see Figure 5.7). For this kind of organizer, you can pose general questions and have students find the answers in the different texts. You can have some groups find answers in one text and other groups find answers in a different text. Intermediate-grade students can directly quote from the texts and use citations. This gives students an opportunity to see how they can use information from more than one text to come up with good answers to questions posed about a topic in which they read multiple texts to find the answers. Combining this information helps students learn more about a given topic than they would through reading just one text. In addition, students can see how different texts cover the same subject in different ways.

Sequencing Graphic Organizers. This graphic organizer helps students identify events or facts in a sequence (see Figure 5.8). Students who read multiple texts have the advantage of having more than one text to draw from as they determine the sequence of events that take place. Students can either paraphrase the text or use direct quotes as in Figure 5.7. Students also will benefit from learning different signal words that cue readers into this particular text structure (Figure 5.9).

Cause-and-Effect Graphic Organizers. Several different graphic organizers can depict cause and effect. As students consider an event like the Titanic sinking, cause and effect become very important concepts for identifying what happened and why. While you could use a

Figure 5.7. Questions and Answers About the _Titanic_

Question: At the moment when the Titanic hit the iceberg, what did the passengers feel?		
Titanic 1—_TITANIC Disaster at Sea_ (Jenkins & Sanders, 2008)	**Titanic 2—_Titanic Survivor Esther Bloomfield Hart Recalls Tragic Sinking_**	**Titanic 3—_The Sinking of the Titanic: Excerpts from an Eyewitness Account_**
1. "...feeling as if the ship had just run over a thousand marbles." (p. 23) 2. "Lucy Duff Gordon said it was as though someone had drawn a giant finger along the ship's side." (p. 23)	Esther Hall: "a dreadful tearing ripping sound—the sound of great masses of steel and iron being violently torn, rent and cut asunder."	Harold Bride: "I hardly knew it had happened after the Captain had come to us. There was no jolt whatever."
Conclusion from passenger responses: Passengers felt and heard different things at varying degrees when the ship hit the iceberg. What the passengers heard may have depended on where they were located on the ship.		

Figure 5.8. Sequencing Timeline of the *Titanic* After the Iceberg Hit

| The Titanic comes to a stop. | → | Cold water begins to pour into the ship. | → | Passengers were given life jackets. |

Figure 5.9. Signal Words for Sequencing Structure

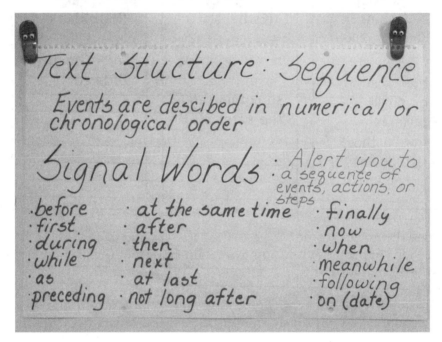

sequence-of-events organizer to show what happened, as we did in Figure 5.8, the sequence of events in itself does not clearly identify what happened as a result of a specific cause. Thus, sometimes it is more useful to use a cause/effect structure to identify what happened and why. For example, we can read the different accounts of the sinking of the *Titanic* and determine the causes and effects of that event, as we show in Figure 5.10.

Problem/Solution Graphic Organizers. Problem/solution is another text structure that students can find useful when they compare and contrast multiple informational texts, especially those in social studies and science. Students can look at an event and interpret it through a problem/solution structure to determine what the problems were and

Figure 5.10. Cause/Effect Graphic Organizer for *Titanic*

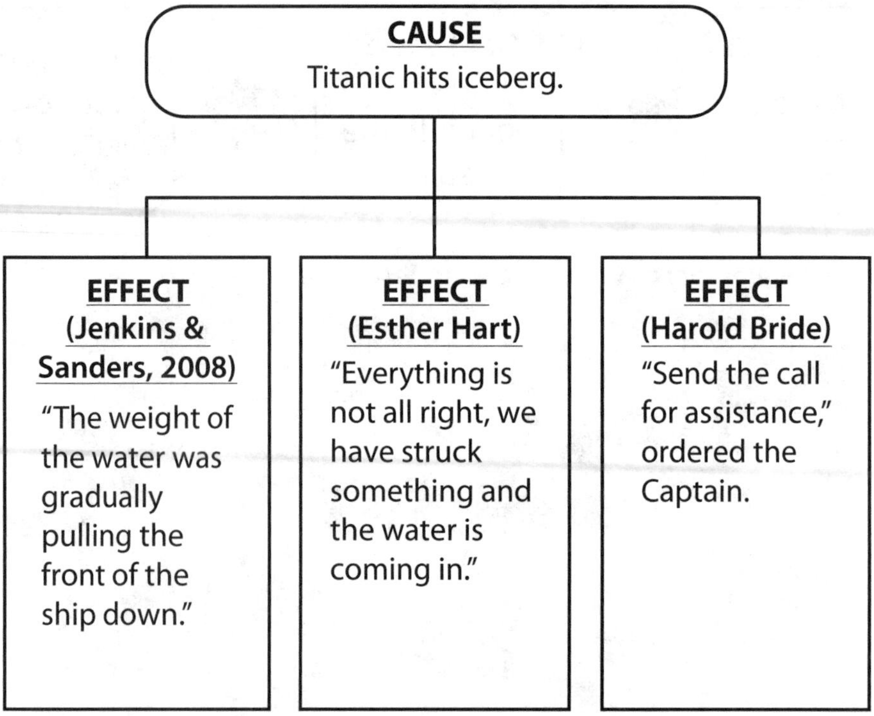

how they were solved. If we look at the sinking of the *Titanic* through the lens of problem/solution, we might construct the graphic organizer shown in Figure 5.11.

Compare/Contrast Graphic Organizers. Finally, graphic organizers help students with the compare/contrast text structure. This structure lies at the heart of Standard 9, and there are many different ways that the compare/contrast structure can be represented graphically (Figures 5.12, 5.13). Each way helps students distill the important information from the multiple texts they read.

Answering Text-Dependent Questions

Chapter 4 discussed the value and purpose of answering text-dependent questions for narrative texts. Text-dependent questions are also an important way to help readers read and understand multiple informational texts. As with narrative texts, teachers can use Webb's DOK Taxonomy (Webb, 2002) and the four levels of questions that the taxonomy promotes to develop all kinds of questions that would be appropriate for informational texts. For example, using the many verbs the DOK identifies, teachers can ask such questions as:

Figure 5.11. Problem/Solution Graphic Organizer for *Titanic*

Problem		Solution
1. The *Titanic* started to sink.	→	a. The watertight doors in the bulkheads had begun to close. (Jenkins & Sanders, 2008)
		b. "All the men are at the lifeboats . . ." (Esther Hart)
2. The passengers knew that they must abandon ship.	→	a. "Their job was to ensure that the boats were manned, load passengers into them, and see them safely launched, while at the same time keeping order and making sure that panic did not break out." (Jenkins & Sanders, 2008)
		b. "I heard the hoarse shouts of 'Women and children first,' and then from boat to boat we were hurried, only to be told 'already full.'" (Esther Hart)
		c. "Then came the Captain's voice: 'Men, you have done your full duty. You can do no more. Abandon your cabin. Now it's every man for himself.'" (Harold Bride)
		d. "I walked back to Phillips. I said the last raft was gone." (Harold Bride)

Figure 5.12. Venn Diagram of Two Firsthand Accounts of the Sinking of the *Titanic*

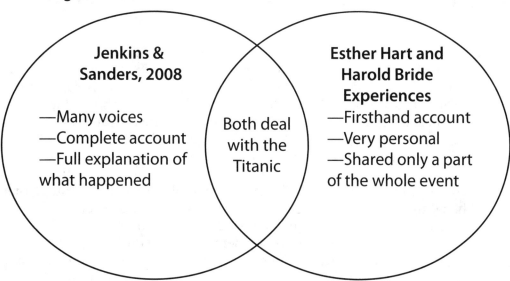

Jenkins & Sanders, 2008

—Many voices
—Complete account
—Full explanation of what happened

Both deal with the Titanic

Esther Hart and Harold Bride Experiences
—Firsthand account
—Very personal
—Shared only a part of the whole event

Figure 5.13. Compare/Contrast Organizer for Two Accounts of the Sinking of the *Titanic*

Jenkins & Sanders, 2008	Esther Hart Account
• Presents many voices of passengers and crew members • Gives a detailed account of the whole event, from when the *Titanic* was designed and built to the aftermath of the event and its effects on future ships	• Presents voice of Esther Hart in a personal narrative account of her experiences on board the *Titanic* • Gives a personal narrative of the time just prior to when Esther boarded the *Titanic* until she was rescued by another ship.

Jenkins & Sanders, and Hart

• Both give quotes from the passengers who were there when the *Titanic* sank.

• Both show the personal anguish and fright of the passengers.

"Recall the two main ideas presented in both texts. Compare and contrast these ideas."

"Compare and contrast the details that support each main idea. How are they the same and how are they different?"

Figures 5.14, 5.15, and 5.16 address the types of text-dependent questions teachers can ask about informational texts using the CCSS's three dimensions of Key Ideas and Details, Craft and Structure, and Integration of Knowledge and Ideas.

Getting the Gist

Vaughn and her colleagues (Klingner & Vaughn, 1998; Klingner, Vaughn, & Schumm, 1998; Vaughn, Klingner, & Bryant, 2001) have developed a simple strategy for helping students get the gist of a short article or informational text (Figure 5.17). This strategy is part of their project called Collaborative Strategic Reading (CSR) (http://www.readingrockets.org/article/103/). The Getting the Gist strategy especially helps younger readers and lower-achieving readers who have difficulty with the more complex strategy of summarizing texts.

Getting the gist involves getting the key idea of a text. It is a less complex task than summarizing, for example, but it is a strategy that helps students focus on the main idea of a text. We see getting the gist as a simple strategy that introduces the idea of summarizing to young readers especially and to older readers who have difficulty learning the rules for summarizing. While getting the gist will not be sufficient for intermediate-grade students, it is a start.

Figure 5.14. Compare-and-Contrast Questions about Key Ideas and Details in Multiple Informational Texts

- Compare and contrast the main ideas and details about the topic of each text.

- Compare and contrast the central ideas and how each author develops those central ideas.

- Summarize each text. Compare and contrast your summaries. How are they the same and how are they different?

- Analyze how an event, person, or idea is introduced, illustrated, and elaborated in each text. How are the introduction, illustrations, and elaborations the same and different across texts?

- Compare and contrast how each text makes connections among and distinctions between ideas, individuals, and events.

- Compare and contrast the textual evidence each text uses to support its claims and ideas.

- Compare and contrast the different inferences that you can draw from each text. How are they the same and how are they different?

Figure 5.15. Compare-and-Contrast Questions about Craft and Structure Using Multiple Texts

- Compare and contrast the way each author lets you know the most important concepts or words in each text.

- Compare and contrast how each author gets the reader's attention at the beginning of each piece.

- How and why does each author use white space between paragraphs and sections of each text? How does that help readers?

- Compare and contrast how each author defines words for readers. What do they do?

- Compare and contrast how each author lets you know the topic of a section of a passage. How does each author let know what a passage will be about?

- Compare and contrast each author's use of the various signal or cue words, like "First," "next," and "last." How do those words help you as a reader?

- Compare and contrast each author's use of illustrations at different points in time. How do those illustrations help you as readers?

- How do the illustrations and captions help the reader understand each text better?

- Does each author use arrows and captions along with the illustrations? How do these help readers?

Figure 5.15. Compare-and-Contrast Questions about Craft and Structure Using Multiple Texts (continued)

- What are some words each author uses to show contrast?
- What are some words each author uses that help tell readers the author's viewpoint? Compare and contrast the way each author lets readers know his or her viewpoint.

Figure 5.16. Compare and Contrast the Integration of Knowledge and Ideas from Multiple Informational Texts

- Compare and contrast the most important points presented by two texts on the same topic.
- Compare and contrast how each author uses the same evidence to present the author's viewpoint about the topic.
- Compare and contrast how each author presents information which conflicts directly with what the other author presents.
- Compare and contrast the different conclusions each author draws about events, a person, or an idea.
- Compare and contrast a personal account with a textbook account of an event, a person, or an idea.
- Integrate information from two texts on the same topic in order to speak and write about the topic knowledgeably.

Self-Questioning

Of the many different comprehension strategies, self-questioning has been shown to be one of the most effective for students (NICHD, 2000). The who-what-when-where-why? Self-questioning strategy is an excellent one that provides important basic information that students should get out of any informational text they read. Teachers have used 3 x 5 cards held together with a single metal ring holder to provide a manipulative that students can use for this strategy. On the ring, they place five cards, each with one of the questions along with a question mark. They color-code each question so that they can identify the questions through the color. Each student gets a full set of the cards. As students read an informational text, they ask and answer the five basic questions based on what they read. This strategy works well when students are paired up and can ask themselves questions and answer them aloud to their partners.

Using the self-questioning strategy helps students work to understand each individual text they read. They can use the answers to their questions as a foundation for some of the more difficult kinds of questions that we recommended earlier in this chapter. For example, with the Jenkins and Sanders (2008) and the Bride texts on the *Titanic*,

Figure 5.17. Getting the Gist

1. Who or what is this piece about?

   _____

   _____

2. What happened to the who or what?

   _____

   _____

   _____

3. Say it in 10 words or less.

   _____

   _____

   _____

students can begin a comparison and contrast between the two texts simply by looking at their responses to the who-what-when-where-why questions as seen on Figure 5.18. They then have the basic information—key ideas and details—to evaluate the texts more carefully.

Another strategy students can use for self-questioning is the Elaborative-Integration strategy (Menke & Pressley, 1994; Woloshyn, Pressley, & Schneider, 1992). This strategy is characterized by the use of "why" questions. Students read a sentence or paragraph and then ask "why?" They then try to answer the question by integrating the new information they just read with their background knowledge. For example, if they read this paragraph about the *Titanic*:

> Harold Bride, the wireless operator of the sunken liner, told how, just before the ship went down, the band on deck was playing 'Autumn.' The

Figure 5.18. Self-Questioning of the Jenkins & Sanders (2008) and Bride Texts

Question	Jenkins and Sanders (2008) Text	Harold Bride Text
Who?	Crew and passengers of the Titanic	One employee on the ship, Harold Bride
What?	An account of the final hours of the Titanic	Harold's account of his experiences signaling for help, getting from the ship to a lifeboat, and being rescued
When?	From the designing and building of the Titanic until after the event happened	From when the iceberg hit to the time Harold was rescued
Where?	On the Atlantic and in America	On the Atlantic and in a lifeboat
Why?	To present an overall account of what happened according to the crew and passengers on the ship	To tell readers about his personal experiences and reactions to the events of the Titanic

song 'Autumn' occurs in an Episcopalian hymn book, and, as will be readily seen, there are many things in it that would fit appropriately the situation on the Titanic in the last moments of pain and darkness there. One line, "Hold me up in mighty waters," particularly may have suggested the hymn to some minister aboard the doomed vessel, who, it has been suggested, thereupon asked the remaining passengers to join in singing the hymn, in a last service aboard the sinking ship, soon to be ended by death itself. (http://www.encyclopedia-titanica.org/sinking-ships-band-chose-fitting-hymn-11707.html)

Students ask, "Why did the band on deck play the song 'Autumn'?" This is an excellent question to get students to think deeply about the tragedy of the *Titanic* and the symbolism of the song to the unfolding tragic events. For more information about this strategy, see https://k12teacherstaffdevelopment.com/tlb/what-is-the-elaborative-interrogation-strategy/.

Using Tools as Supports

In addition to the many graphic organizers teachers can use to help students compare and contrast multiple informational texts, they can also make available to students many other kinds of tools similar to those recommended for narrative texts. When teaching students to read across complex informational texts, it helps them if teachers use many different supports to help them look deeply at two or more texts.

Offline supports for informational texts are similar to those used with narratives. When teachers want students to reread a given text and think deeply about it, it is important to make copies of the texts that students can mark up with pencils, markers, crayons, and highlighters. They can also use sticky notes to identify particular points in the text where they find answers to questions or to find a specific quote that answers a question. They can use markers to highlight or circle concept words that are relevant to the topic or idea. They can use highlighters to identify evidence that proves a point. These types of activities are the kinds students will be required to do on the new online assessments that are computer-based. Performing these skills with real texts is a starting point to help students perform these skills online.

Tech-savvy students are increasingly going online to research information, and online support tools can be used as students are reading and researching information about topics, issues, people, and places of interest to them. These include the use of:

- different colors of highlighting to focus attention on the most important information
- bookmarking to remember specific sites that have relevant information
- marginal notes on some programs, where students can add notes to what they read
- search engines like Google for looking up information
- Wikipedia for gaining initial insight or definitions
- online dictionaries and thesauruses for word meanings, synonyms, and antonyms
- maps, charts, illustrations, graphs, and photographs
- primary sources for history and science
- Ask.com

K–5 students have never had more support tools to learn about and study different topics than they do now. These materials are critically important for students to be aware of and learn from as they progress through school. Early elementary school is the best time to start.

SUMMARY

> As the name implies, informational text is text that provides information and is generally more difficult to read than narrative text. Factors that contribute to these texts being more difficult include unfamiliar content, new vocabulary that denotes specific concepts, and the varied types of text structure.

➢ Knowing the structure of a text helps students identify the main ideas and details of informational texts.

➢ One of the main purposes for reading multiple texts is to expand students' understanding of a topic. In addition to reading printed text, students need to read and interpret information presented digitally and graphically.

➢ As with narrative text, students benefit from having the ability to apply strategies while reading informational text. One such strategy is the use of graphic organizers. Such organizers include question/answer, sequencing, cause and effect, problem/solution, and compare/contrast.

➢ Other strategies that support multiple informational texts include having students answer text-dependent questions of varying levels, summarizing text, self-questioning, and researching information from online resources.

CHAPTER 6

Knowledge-Building Across Multiple Texts

This chapter is intended to help teachers think about and build lessons and units based on Reading Anchor Standard 9: "Analyze how two or more texts address similar themes or topics in order to build knowledge . . ." An introduction to this topic can best begin with a story of two 1st-grade teachers who worked down the hall from one another. One teacher, let's call her Ms. Merlon, conducted a unit on teddy bears. She had her 1st-graders bring in teddy bears they owned and cherished. Children drew teddy bears. They conducted show-and-tell about their teddy bears. Ms. Merlon read aloud stories like *The Teddy Bear* (McPhail, 2005) and *Teddy Bear's Picnic* (Kennedy & Day, 2000). She had a bulletin board displaying pictures of the children's teddy bears along with their written stories about their teddy bears.

Across the hall, Ms. Springer also conducted a unit on bears. Her unit, however, looked very different from Ms. Merlon's. Ms. Springer wanted her students to learn about bears. Her bulletin board was covered with pictures of different kinds of bears—black bears, brown bears, polar bears, and panda bears. Each bear was placed within its habitat and the geographic area where it lived, the type of food it ate, its behaviors, its hibernation patterns, and so forth. Instead of teddy bear books, Ms. Springer used the Internet to show students all kinds of videos about bears. She read books like *Pandas! A Kids Book About Pandas* (Shye, 2013), *Bears: Amazing Pictures and Fun Facts on Animals in Nature* (de Silva, 2013), and *Bears: Polar Bears, Black Bears and Grizzly Bears* (Hodge & Stephens, 1996). She also read a few fun literary books like *Bear Snores On* (Wilson & Chapman, 2005) and *Brown Bear, Brown Bear, What Do You See?* (Martin, 1996). Ms. Springer's children were as excited and enthusiastic as they could be. They wrote stories, drew pictures, read more books, and saw videos and Internet pictures of bears. They compared different types of bears with one another. Further, they wanted to talk to everyone who came into their classroom about what they were learning about bears.

The contrast between what Ms. Merlon's and Ms. Springer's children were learning was startling and best represents the meaning of this chapter. Ms. Merlon's children were celebrating what they already knew, but Ms. Springer's children were building their knowledge base and their world knowledge about bears. They were highly engaged with their learning and having a great time. They loved learning about bears. And their knowledge base grew, laying a foundation for further learning in intermediate, middle, and high school.

READING TO BUILD KNOWLEDGE

Recall Reading Anchor Standards 7 and 9 (Figure 6.1). These standards highlight two critical issues for this book, (1) integrating knowledge and ideas from multiple print and digital sources, and (2) integrating knowledge and ideas to build more knowledge.

The focus of this chapter is to help you think about why and how to use multiple print and digital sources to build knowledge. We begin by looking at what research tells us about how students build and use background knowledge.

The Development of Background Knowledge

Background knowledge has an interesting relationship to reading in general and particularly to reading across multiple texts. Teachers know the critical importance of background knowledge for reading comprehension. This importance has been known for some 50 years—the more you know about a given topic, the better your comprehension of a text on that topic (Anderson & Pearson, 1984; Neuman, 2006; Recht & Leslie, 1988; Spilich, Vesonder, Chiesi, & Voss, 1979; Willingham, 2006). But, interestingly, the CCSS has focused us on the reciprocal part of the relationship between background knowledge and reading comprehension, because, in fact, reading across multiple texts is one important way to *build* background knowledge about a topic on which students do not have much knowledge (Adams, 2010/2011; Guthrie, Anderson, Alao, & Rinehart, 1999). So the relationship between background knowledge and comprehension is reciprocal—the more you know, the better your comprehension, but the more you read, the more you know.

Before we discuss how important building background knowledge is to reading across multiple texts, we want to share what researchers

Figure 6.1. Reading Anchor Standards for Informational Texts

Anchor Standard 7 for Informational Texts: Integrate and evaluate content presented in diverse media and formats, including visually and quantitatively, as well as in words.

Anchor Standard 9 for Informational Texts: Compare and contrast the major points and key details in two texts on the same topic.

have learned over the last 50 years about why background knowledge is so important.

Most teachers ask students to talk about their background knowledge before they read a text or before they introduce new knowledge that they want students to learn. This is an excellent practice for several reasons, one of which is because teachers know that they can engage students in their reading and learning by talking about what they already know. While teachers know that building background knowledge is important, it can be helpful to think for a minute why this is so, and the role that it plays in teaching and learning.

In its most general sense, background knowledge refers to all the existing knowledge an individual holds in memory. Usually, background knowledge is knowledge an individual possesses about various topics. For example, one might characterize all of the knowledge one holds about mountains as one's background knowledge about mountains. This knowledge would include all the individual concepts one holds about mountains; all of one's experiences in and with mountains; related knowledge about hills, valleys, canyons, and plateaus; and so forth. Someone who lives in the Rocky Mountains may have what cognitive psychologists call deep knowledge about mountains, and would likely know the difference between a valley and a canyon, and be able to identify and draw a plateau. On the other hand, someone who lives by the ocean and has never traveled far beyond might have far less background knowledge, perhaps even a superficial knowledge, about mountains. Regardless of whether knowledge is deep or superficial, it is still considered background knowledge.

Students cannot call to mind and work with background knowledge they do not have (Bransford, 1979; Neuman, 2006). If high school students have limited experiences with mountains, then they cannot call to mind their mountain knowledge base when they read about tectonic plates and their movements. This may limit to some extent the rich and deep knowledge students can develop about the movement of plates and the resulting geographic events caused by such movements. Of course, most students have many vicarious experiences with mountains, such as seeing pictures, movies, and videos showing mountains. But this is not the same experience as students who actually can see the uplifted landmass forms and the striated lines cut across the Earth's surface. The learning will be different; the remembering will be different.

There is another important role that background knowledge plays in learning and school. Students' existing knowledge serves as a filter to interpret what they see, hear, read, and experience in their lives, including their school lives (Anderson, 1984). In other words, students bring to school existing knowledge about many things, and they use this knowledge as a filter to interpret, understand, and remember what they learn in school. This includes, importantly, reading.

This knowledge can be seen in a relatively simple sentence like, "He was already exhausted when he entered the Death Zone." Most adult readers could infer that the Death Zone must mean something bad. But knowledge might still be superficial and limited. One might not know, for example, that the "he" must be a high-altitude mountain climber, or that the Death Zone is anyplace on a mountain above 26,000 feet. Most wouldn't know that there are 14 mountains on earth that are above 26,000 feet, or that humans cannot sustain life above this level and that the body begins to deteriorate. Many would know that oxygen gets thinner on mountains but not that above the Death Zone, the oxygen is about one-third what it is at sea level. So, with this limited oxygen, humans cannot sustain life; they will die. Since this mountain climber is already exhausted, he is in real trouble once he enters the Death Zone.

So we can see that knowledge is a critical part of reading and comprehension. Moreover, it is deep knowledge, such as the knowledge about what the Death Zone represents, that leads to good comprehension. Superficial knowledge most often does not.

Superficial Versus Deep Knowledge

In the early work on knowledge-building, researchers examined individuals who had deep knowledge about something and compared them to their peers who had superficial knowledge. Early studies used expert chess players as those with deep knowledge about chess and compared these expert chess players to novice chess players (Chase & Simon, 1973; Chi, Feltovich, & Glaser, 1981). They found many differences between the two groups. Experts had more knowledge, of course. But experts also had more *organized* knowledge than novices. Also, experts focused on the underlying principles of a given problem rather than its superficial features (Willingham, 2006).

What does deep knowledge look like in students? Perhaps another example will clarify the difference between deep and superficial knowledge. Many young children have limited experiences with restaurants and therefore a rather superficial knowledge about them. On the other hand, most American adults have what we call deep knowledge about restaurants. What is the difference? Most young children have been to a McDonald's or Burger King and know about ordering food at the counter, paying for it there, then picking it up and bringing it back to tables in the restaurant. If you asked them what a restaurant was, they might not be able to define the most important characteristics of a restaurant—a place where you go and people bring you food, and you have to pay for the food—but they are likely to name one or more restaurants like McDonald's or Burger King. Some of them have also had experiences with other types of restaurants where you are seated at a table and a waitress takes your order, delivers your food, and gives you a check. Children may know that you have to pay for the food, but they are unlikely to know that you can pay with a credit card or cash but not with checks. Only adults know that most restaurants don't take checks anymore. Twenty years ago they did, but they tend not to nowadays because of so much check fraud.

As you look at the differences between what children know about restaurants and what adults know, there is a huge chasm. Adults know when you are likely to pay cash (at McDonald's) and when you are likely to pay with a credit card (a more expensive restaurant). Adults know what hostesses are and what they do; they know the difference between a host or hostess, a busboy, and a waiter or waitress. Adults know different ethnic restaurants and what kinds of food those restaurants serve. Adults know different prices of food at restaurants and can distinguish among cafés, buffets, cafeterias, fast-food restaurants, takeouts and elegant restaurants. Many adults know to beware of restaurants where the menus do not include a food price; these are generally the most expensive restaurants. Most children do not know many of these rather simple facts about restaurants.

Another example of defining differences in superficial and deep knowledge is reflected in the differences between the knowledge that experienced teachers have compared to preservice teachers. Berliner (1986) conducted a very interesting study years ago with laypeople and novice and experienced teachers. In this study Berliner asked each of the three groups to view a slide of a classroom for a very brief period of time. Then he asked laypeople and teachers to talk about what they saw.

The important point about the differences among the laypeople, novice, and experienced teachers in this study is that the laypeople and novice teachers could only report what they saw; their reports were basically surface-level descriptions of the classroom, including things like desks, books, and students. The experienced teachers, however, were able to make inferences and elaborations based on what they saw. They reported things like how students were grouped together, what might become problems in the classroom, and what students were likely working on. They applied their specific knowledge about teaching to make sense of the classroom they observed. They were able to go beyond a surface description of what they saw and elaborate on what they saw. Further, their elaboration involved combining and integrating the knowledge gleaned from the slide with their background knowledge.

This is the important point: Students build their knowledge base when they combine and integrate new information they are learning with their background knowledge. This, then, is another example of the difference between surface knowledge and deep knowledge.

How do we know the level of knowledge students have about a topic? An example worth thinking about is when teachers ask students to elaborate in their oral and/or written work. At some point in time, most teachers have asked students to elaborate on what they said or wrote, perhaps without using the word "elaborate," but asking, "tell me more." Sometimes teachers say this at show-and-tell, or when students have written a good topic sentence and then moved right on to a new topic. Individuals can only elaborate when they know a lot about a subject or topic. It is very difficult to elaborate on something you don't know much about.

The ability to elaborate comes from deep knowledge about a subject or topic. Often our students do know a lot about a subject or topic, but they don't elaborate on it. However, they can if they are asked. On the other hand, students can't elaborate on a topic about which they have superficial knowledge.

So, one of the important goals of Standard 9 is to assist students in building their knowledge and developing deep knowledge about the world through reading multiple texts (Figure 6.2). This is our goal. This is where we want our students to go.

Knowledge and Strategies

Throughout this book the teaching of strategies to help students develop an understanding of multiple texts has been encouraged. For many of the lessons and units in this book, students will need to use multiple strategies to help them work across more than one text. At this point, it is useful to consider the relationship between knowledge and strategies in the whole scheme of reading. The difference between teaching knowledge and strategies is one of the most important topics for reading instruction at the K–5 level.

Both knowledge and strategies are critically important to teach. There are literally hundreds of studies that have been conducted over the last 50 years showing the importance of both. Most studies have focused on one or the other. Interestingly, only a few studies have pitted knowledge and strategies against each other (McKeown, Beck, & Blake, 2009).

However, research has shown that a strong knowledge base can make up for a lack of strategies (Alexander, 2002; Alexander & Judy, 1988; Murphy & Alexander, 2002). On the other hand, strong strategies cannot make up for a lack of knowledge. One has only to think of

Figure 6.2. Developing Deep Knowledge About Fish

reading a graduate-level chemistry text to know the truth of this point. In all likelihood, a reader would have a difficult time understanding a graduate-level chemistry text despite having sufficient, even excellent, reading strategies.

The point is not that reading strategies are not important, or that we ought not to teach them. Strategies are very important. And we need to teach them, as demonstrated in this book. However, strategies cannot make up for a paucity of background knowledge. This tells us why we need to focus on building our students' deep knowledge about their world and how it works. No amount of strategy instruction can take the place of deep knowledge. Now the question is, "How do teachers help students build deep knowledge?"

How to Build Deep Knowledge

Now let's go back to how to teach students to build deep knowledge through reading multiple texts. One might reasonably ask, "Well, if background knowledge is so important to reading comprehension, then why don't we just build deep background knowledge?" Well, we can and should be building deep background knowledge. And one of the most important ways to do this is through reading across multiple texts. Adams (2010/2011) shows us how to do this.

In "Advancing Our Students' Language and Literacy," Adams (2010/2011) argues that, "a great benefit of a common core curriculum is that it [will] drive an overhaul of the texts we give students to read, and the kinds of learning and thought we expect their reading to support" (p. 10). Her argument directly relates to the goal of reading across multiple texts to build deep knowledge. She recommends that teachers select a topic about which they want their students to learn and then find many books on that topic. For lower-ability readers, the books should be shorter and simpler. Even when working with average and higher-achieving readers, it is better to begin with easier texts if students completely lack background knowledge. However, a caveat to giving high-achieving readers too-easy text is that they can often thrive on more difficult text (Chall & Conrad, 1991; Kintsch, 2004). Nevertheless, Adams's idea is to start with easy texts on a topic, since students may be unfamiliar with the concepts, ideas, and vocabulary about that topic.

As students are reading easier texts (including online materials, videos, and pictures) on a given topic, teachers begin to teach the main concepts and key ideas about the topic along with the accompanying vocabulary. With this basic knowledge students can begin to read more and harder texts on that topic. Adams (2010/2011) argues that as students read more, they gradually build deeper knowledge about the topic along with related subtopics and unique vocabulary. As they progress, they can handle more difficult and more complex texts on that topic because of their growing background knowledge and corresponding vocabulary.

Adams (2010/2011) uses the example of 2nd-graders who love dinosaurs. She takes her ideas from a fascinating study conducted many years ago by Chi (1978). Chi studied the deep knowledge that some young children have about dinosaurs. These children know the different types of dinosaurs. They can pronounce and recite their names and characteristics. They know which are herbivores and which are carnivores. Because of their deep knowledge about dinosaurs, these children can read and understand texts far beyond their early reading level.

The argument and recommendation that Adams (2010/2011) makes is that teachers can build their students' knowledge base and depth of knowledge about the world through the reading of multiple texts on a given topic.

PRIMARY-GRADE KNOWLEDGE-BUILDING EXAMPLE

This next template (Figure 6.3) and set of lessons present a primary-grade example of how to build background knowledge based on reading two texts about spiders, a topic in which primary-grade students

Figure 6.3. *Spiders* Template

Planning	***Text 1:*** *Spinning Spiders* (Berger, 2003) ☐ Literary ✓ Informational
	Text 2: *Spiders* (Bishop, 2007) ☐ Literary ✓ Informational
	Grade-Level Standard (Lesson Objective): Identify basic similarities in and differences between two texts on the same topic.
	Writing Prompt Question: What can we learn about spiders from reading more than one book about them?
	Strategy: Compare and contrast information.

	Text 1: *Spinning Spiders*	Text 2: *Spiders*
Text Analysis	WHAT SPIDERS LOOK LIKE • Different colors • Big and small • 8 legs • 2 body parts • Spinnerets • Many eyes SPIDER HABITAT • Everywhere • Indoors and outdoors • Trees and grass WHAT AND HOW SPIDERS EAT • Flies • Inject poison drink food • Insects • Birds, frogs	WHAT SPIDERS LOOK LIKE • Hairs that feel movement • 8 legs • 8 eyes • 2 body parts • Spinnerets • Hard skin SPIDER HABITAT • Flowers • Leaves WHAT AND HOW SPIDERS EAT • Meat • Insects • Taste with feet • Injects venom–sucks food

Writing	***Text/Sentence Frame*** (scaffolded response to writing prompt): Both books say that spiders _____ and _____. In the Bishop *Spiders* book, we also learned that _____. In *Spinning Spiders*, we learned that _____.

are perpetually interested. In these lessons, note the use of an online video by Bill Nye the Science Guy that provides a nice introduction to the topic of spiders.

Lesson—Spiders

Grades 1–2

TEXT 1   Berger, M. (2003). *Spinning Spiders*. New York, NY: HarperCollins.

1. Show the covers of both books. Read the objectives with students. Tell students that they are going to learn about spiders by reading two books about spiders. Tell them that the more books they read about spiders, the more they will learn and know about spiders. They will see if the books have the same information about spiders or if the books have additional or different information about spiders.

2. Begin with a video by Bill Nye. Show the first minutes of the video: http://www.youtube.com/watch?v=pF-lEpEquGM.

3. Ask students what they know about spiders. Record students' responses on the board.

4. After students share their knowledge of spiders, tell them that as they read the two books, they will answer the following posted questions:
   a. What do spiders look like?
   b. Where do spiders live?
   c. What and how do spiders eat?
   d. Why do spiders spin silk?

5. Read and discuss each page of *Spinning Spiders*. As each page is read, chart/note any information that answers the questions (Figure 6.3).

After Reading

1. Review the answers to the four questions. Distribute a graphic organizer with the four questions (Figure 6.4). Have students draw a picture in each box and record information they learned from *Spinning Spiders* to answer each question.

TEXT 2   Bishop, N. (2007). *Spiders*. New York, NY: Scholastic.

This text is available in two versions. The first version is the complete text to be used as a read-aloud (ISBN-10: 0439877563; ISBN-13: 978-0439877565). The second version is written at the grade1-2 level (ISBN-10: 0545237572; ISBN-13: 978-0545237574).

Figure 6.4. *Spiders* **Graphic Organizer**

SPIDERS	
Name_____	
What do spiders look like?	What and how do spiders eat?
Where do spiders live?	Why do spiders spin silk?

1. Review the objectives. Review previously recorded information charted from *Spinning Spiders* (see Figure 6.3).
2. Read Bishop's *Spiders*. Choose one version to read to or with the students. Chart answers to the same four questions (see Figure 6.3). Ask students to compare the illustrations from Text 1 to the photographs in Text 2. Which portrays a more realistic image of spiders? What are the characterstics of the illustration that make the image more realistic?

After Reading

1. Review the information recorded on the chart for *Spinning Spiders* (Figure 6.3). Ask students what additional information they learned from the Bishop text.
2. Look at each question separately and discuss the information that was the same in both books. Ask students to identify the information that was included in only one book. Stress that if they had read only one of the books, they would not have learned the information in the other book. Ask students what information would have been missed if only one book had been read? Instruct students to look at the graphic organizer they completed for Text 1 (Figure 6.4) and add any additional information to their pictures or words.

Writing

Use Figure 6.5 to compare and contrast what students learned in both books about spiders that can be used to answer each of the four questions. Again, remind students that reading more books about a topic provides additional information about the topic.

Figure 6.5. Compare and Contrast Spider Information

	Spinning Spiders	**BOTH BOOKS**	*Spiders*
What do spiders look like?	Different colors Big and small	8 legs 2 body parts Spinneret	Hairs that feel movement 8 eyes Hard skin
Where do spiders live?	Everywhere Indoors and out-doors Trees and grass	Plants	Flowers Leaves
What and how do spi-ders eat?	Flies Insects Birds, frogs, liz-ards, fish	Insects Inject poison, drink/suck food	Meat Taste with feet
Why do spiders spin silk?	Spin webs to catch bugs	Webs to catch bugs	Help move around Wrap eggs

---

Written Prompt

What can we learn about spiders from reading more than one book about them?

If students need support and assistance talking and writing about spiders, use the following sentence.

Spiders Sentence Frame

Both books say that spiders _____ and _____. In the Bishop *Spiders* book, we also learned that _____. In *Spinning Spiders*, we learned that _____.

Additional Multimedia Resources

Additional information and resources about spiders may be found at the following websites:

- Kids—International Society for Arachnology: http://arachnology.org/Arachnology/Pages/Kids.html

- Kids Connect—Spiders: http://www.kidskonnect.com/subjectindex/13-categories/animals/51-spiders.html
- North American Spiders: http://www.insectidentification.org/spiders.asp
- Kid Zone: http://www.kidzone.ws/lw/spiders/index.htm
- Types of Spiders: http://www.typesofspiders.net/
- Facts about spiders: http://www.pestworldforkids.org

INTERMEDIATE-GRADE KNOWLEDGE-BUILDING EXAMPLE

The Internet as well as book sources like Amazon.com list and describe many books, articles, first-person accounts, and newspaper and magazine pieces about many social studies and science events, ideas, and concepts. These materials provide a rich database from which to draw on in thinking about and planning how to build students' knowledge. The more knowledge that is built with younger readers, the more these students will know as they enter middle and high school, where knowledge is the first and most important commodity.

In the next set of lessons we present, we want to show you how you can use printed texts, both narrative and informational, as well as multimedia and the Internet, to build knowledge about tsunamis (Figure 6.6).

LESSON—TSUNAMIS

Grades 4–5

TEXT 1   Stiefel, C. (2009). *Tsunamis (A True Book)*. Danbury, CT: Childrens Press.

1. Read and discuss the lesson objectives. Show students the four texts and tell them that they are going to "integrate the information" from multiple texts about tsunamis. Help them understand that using more than one resource to research a topic or answer questions will provide them with more information as well as increase the chance that the information will be more accurate.

2. Content vocabulary: Tell students that as they read the texts, they will compile a list of unusual or uncommon words related to tsunamis. Put a check (✓) by those words encountered in different texts.

3. Activate background knowledge.
   a. Explain that a tsunami is a particular type of wave that can cause a great deal of devastation. Tell students that they will view a YouTube video of a tsunami. As they watch the video, have students write questions they have about tsunamis.

b. Show the first 3 minutes of the YouTube tsunami video: http://www.youtube.com/watch?v=tUN_UTY0GNo

c. Chart the questions generated by students (see Figure 6.7). Consolidate the list to 5 to 6 general questions that they would like to use to guide their research.

Comprehension Strategy Instruction:
Scanning to Find Answers to Student Self-Generated Questions

1. Tell the students that they will learn to look for answers to the class questions by using a strategy called Scanning for Information (see Chapter 4). Use the procedure of Scanning for Information (Figure 4.18) and the *Tsunamis* book (Text 1) to explicitly teach scanning. Possible examples:

    a. Ask students to identify the key word in question 2 (What causes tsunamis?). Once they have determined the keyword as "causes," have

Figure 6.6. *Tsunami* **Template**

	Text 1: Tsunamis (Stiefel, 2009) ☐ Literary ✓ Informational
	Text 2: Tsunami (www.enchantedlearning.com/subjects/tsunami/) ☐ Literary ✓ Informational
	Text 3: Tsunami! (Kajikawa, 2009) ✓ Literary ☐ Informational
	Text 4: The Big Wave (Buck, 1947) ✓ Literary ☐ Informational
Planning	*Grade-Level Standard* (Lesson Objective): **RL5.9** Compare and contrast stories in the same genre on their approaches to similar themes and topics. **RI5.7.** Draw on information from multiple print or digital sources, demonstrating the ability to locate an answer to a question quickly or to solve a problem efficiently. **RI5.9.** Integrate information from several texts on the same topic in order to write or speak about the subject knowledgeably.
	Writing Prompt Question: What different information do we learn from reading multiple texts about tsunamis?
	Strategy: Scanning for information; compare and contrast information.

Figure 6.6. *Tsunami* Template (continued)

	Question		*Answer*
Text Analysis	1. What are tsunamis?	Text 1	Series of huge waves triggered by a sudden movement of the ocean floor Some waves reached as high as 55 feet
		Text 2	A series of huge waves Tsunamis cause devastation and can kill people At landfall, a tsunami wave can be hundreds of meters tall
		Text 3	Grandfather: "Tsunami-monster wave." All stared at the destruction below. The village had disappeared.
		Text 4	The wave "rushed over the flat still of the ocean..." and "reached the village and covered it fathoms deep in swirling wild water, green laced with fierce white foam." Jiya's family and home were gone.
	2. What causes tsunamis?	Text 1	Earthquakes (shift in tectonic plates) Volcanoes, asteroids, and landslides
		Text 2	Earthquakes, volcanoes, and asteroids, rock slide
		Text 3	Grandfather: "An earthquake is coming."
		Text 4	Earthquake/volcano "Steam burst out and lifted the ocean high into the sky in a big wave."
	3. Where do tsunamis most often occur?	Text 1	85% of tsunamis occur in the Pacific.
		Text 2	90% of earthquakes occur in the Pacific Ocean.
		Text 3	Setting: Near the sea in Japan
		Text 4	Setting: Village near the sea in Japan

Figure 6.6. *Tsunami* Template (continued)

	Question		Answer
Text Analysis	4. What are the warning signs of a tsunami?	Text 1	Feel earth shake Receding water on shore
		Text 2	If you see the water recede quickly, and unexpectedly from a beach, that means that the water is going out toward the ocean—then run toward higher ground or inland—there may be a tsunami coming (drawback).
		Text 3	Grandfather felt "rumbling underneath his feet." "The sea was running away from the land."
		Text 4	Increased volcanic activity. Kino's father: "Earth and sea are struggling together against the fires inside the earth."
	5. How can we make communities safer?	Text 1	Warning signs Tsunameters (water pressure recorder on ocean floor/buoys) Sirens
		Text 2	Warning signs Computerized offshore buoys System of sirens on the beach to alert people of potential tsunami danger
		Text 3	Grandfather burns fields and priest rings temple bell to warn villagers of eminent danger.
		Text 4	Temple bell ringing
Writing	***Text/Sentence Frame*** (scaffolded response to writing prompt): We learned a lot about tsunamis from reading several texts. From the book *Tsunamis* (Text 1), we learned _____, _____, and _____. In addition to this, we read an online article and learned _____ and _____. This information helped us when we read two fictional stories, *Tsunami!* and *The Big Wave*. For example, when we read _____, it helped to know that _____. The two stories also helped us better understand the effects of tsunami by _____ and _____.		

Figure 6.7. Student Tsunami Questions

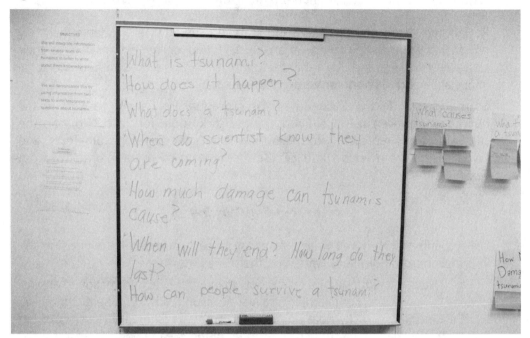

students begin scanning the table of contents. Draw their attention to the entry that refers them to page 7: "What *caused* the 2004 Indian Ocean tsunami?" Next, have them begin scanning on page 7. Once the students have determined that tsunamis are caused by earthquakes (page 9), have a student write "earthquake" on a sticky note and place it under Question 2 on the chart (see Figure 6.8).

b. Remind students to look at headings and pictures for ideas. Scan through the book for headings, pictures, or graphs that might help determine tsunami causes. Draw students' attention to page 19 of the picture of the volcano.

c. Continue with questions 2 and 3 and guide students in finding answers to the questions. Write answers on sticky notes and place them under the appropriate question/category. Assign groups of 2 to 4 students to work on questions 4 and 5.

After Reading

1. Have volunteers read the answers posted under each question.

2. Ask students to identify some important words related to tsunamis to add to the tsunami word list.

TEXT 2   *Tsunami* (www.enchantedlearning.com/subjects/tsunami/)

1. Review the lesson objectives and the scanning strategy. Tell students that they will search another text which is an article found online for answers to their class questions. Remind them that the purpose of this lesson is to find additional information and to check for accuracy of information.

2. Scan and read Text 2. Follow a similar procedure for finding answers to the questions; however, use a different-colored sticky note for Text 2 to help the students visually represent information for "What's the Same in Both Texts" and "What's Different in Texts 1 and 2?" (Be sure to leave room for information from Texts 3 and 4.)

After Reading/Writing

1. Tell students that they will write a response to each question by integrating the information from both texts written on the sticky notes.

    a. Use the first question to model how to integrate the information to answer the questions. For example, the first question reads, "What are tsunamis?" On the first sticky note one student writes, "A tsunami is a series of big waves made by a sudden movement of the ocean floor." A second sticky note reads, "Tsunamis cause devastation and death." Show students how to combine both statements to write, "Tsunamis are huge ocean waves that can cause devastation and death."

    b. Point out discrepancies in information from the two texts as well. For example, two of the sticky notes are about the percentage of tsunamis that occur in the Pacific Ocean. One states 85% and the other states 90%. Tell students that these are not the same numbers but they are relatively close, so they could respond with, "About 85%–90% of tsunamis occur in the Pacific Ocean." Another option would be to tell students to go to a third source to check the information.

    c. Discuss any new vocabulary words from Text 2 and add them to the Tsunami Word List.

TEXT 3   Kajikawa, K. (2009). *Tsunami!* New York, NY: Philomel Books.

TEXT 4   Buck, P. S. (1947). *The Big Wave.* New York, NY: HarperCollins Children's Books.

1. Read the objectives with students. Tell students they will be reading two stories about tsunamis. In both stories the characters are affected by tsunamis. Tell them that these stories were not written to provide facts about tsunamis. However, as they read they should think about the five questions they answered previously.

2. Read Texts 3 and 4. Use story maps to note important elements for each of the narrative stories.

3. Use different-colored sticky notes to add information or insights to the five class questions (Figure 6.8). How did the stories align with the facts learned about tsunamis? What additional insights about tsunamis can be learned from the two stories?

4. Discuss any new vocabulary words from Texts 3 and 4 and add them to the Tsunami Word List.

After Reading

1. Review the responses to the questions (Figure 6.6). Use the following questions to help students integrate facts from the informational texts with the elements of the narrative texts. Discuss how the information about tsunamis helped them better understand each story. Some points to consider:

   a. How did the informational texts about tsunamis help us better understand each story? What did we learn from the two informational texts (Texts 1 and 2) that helps us understand what the author of *Tsunami!* (Text 3) meant when she wrote "the sea was running away from the land." What information from Texts 1 and 2 explains what the author of *The Big*

Figure 6.8. Student Responses to Class-Generated Questions About Tsunamis

Wave (Text 4) meant when she wrote "the earth and sea are struggling together against the fires inside the earth"?

2. Discuss how the experiences of the characters help students better understand tsunamis. Some points to consider:

    a. How do the personal experiences of the characters help us better understand the level of devastation caused by tsunamis? How does this help us develop empathy for people who experience tsunamis? For example, in *The Big Wave* (Text 4) what effect did the tsunami have on the lives of Jiya and Kino and their families? How were their lives different following the tsunami?

    b. How did the characters' knowledge of and previous experiences with tsunamis affect their actions and responses to the situation? For example, in both stories the old men had an understanding of tsunamis. How did this knowledge affect their actions? Compare their actions to the actions of the younger characters. How did the old men in each story warn the people of the imminent danger that was approaching the shores? Why did some characters survive and others did not? What warning systems are available today in countries where tsunamis might occur?

    c. What were the motivations of the different characters in each book? For example, in both stories the old men and the younger characters were motivated by different knowledge and experiences. How did these motivations differ? How did the characters react based on their specific motivations?

    d. How do cultures in which the people have a history of experiencing tsunamis and their warning signs adjust their lifestyles to cope with the possibility of a tsunami? How does this differ from cultures in which tsunamis have been a rare occurrence?

3. Review the list of vocabulary words on the Tsunami Word List.

Writing Prompt

What different information do we learn from reading multiple texts about tsunamis?

Help the students write a paragraph to describe the different information they learned from reading multiple texts about tsunamis.

Tsunami Sentence Frame

The following paragraph may be helpful for some students:

We learned a lot about tsunamis from reading several texts. From the book *Tsunamis,* we learned _____, _____, and _____. In addition to this, we read an online article and learned _____ and _____. This information helped us when we read two fictional stories, *Tsunami!* and *The Big Wave.* For example, when we read _____, it helped to know that _____. The two stories also helped us better understand the effects of tsunamis by _____ and _____.

Additional Multimedia Resources

The following websites offer a wealth of information and resources to extend learning about tsunamis:

- About Weather: weather.about.com/od/weatherinstruments/a/ Tsunamis.htm

- National Geographic Education: http://education. nationalgeographic.com/education/media/tsunamis-101/?ar_a=1; http://education.nationalgeographic.com/education/topics/natural-disasters/?ar_a=1

- National Oceanic and Atmospheric Administration: http://www. tsunami.noaa.gov/; http://www.tsunami.noaa.gov/teacher-resources. html

EXAMPLES OF KNOWLEDGE-BUILDING

Many of the social studies and science units that elementary teachers have traditionally developed for their students are good examples of knowledge-building activities. Teachers design these units to build their students' knowledge about important topics in different subject areas. This knowledge provides the foundation for students' learning of content areas as they enter middle and high school.

One Example: Native American Unit

One example of building knowledge through reading multiple texts comes from a multifaceted unit of study for 5th-grade students about Native Americans. Students read across a wide variety of both informational and narrative texts, including books, e-books, Internet sites, videos, and photo essays. The class developed a large wall display divided into grids, and students used 8-inch-by-6-inch sticky notes to document important information as it was located.

Mr. Olsen used a large collection of informational texts to gradually build students' knowledge about Native Americans. He used the *New True Book Series* (Children's Press), which contain information and photographs from individual tribes such as *The Sioux* (Cunningham, 2011b), *The Navajo* (Cunningham, 2011a), *The Wampanoags* (Cunningham, 2011c), and *The Shawnee* (Flanagan, 1998). Another series he used included titles such as *If You Lived with the Iroquois* (Levine, 1999), *If You Lived with the Sioux* (McGovern, 1992), and *If You Lived with the Cherokees* (Roop, 1998). Additional books included *DK Eyewitness Books: North American Indian* (Murdoch, 2005) and *Indian Nations of North America* (Hill & Frazier, 2010), among many others.

Mr. Olsen and his students also read and compared Native American legends and folktales such as *How the Stars Fell Into the Sky* (Oughton, 1996), *The Girl Who Loved Wild Horses* (Goble, 1993), *Brave Wolf and the Thunderbird* (Crow, Crow, & Martin, 1998), *Raven: A Trickster Tale from the Pacific Northwest* (McDermott, 2001), *Legend of Sleeping Bear* (Wargin, 1998), and a set of Native American plays, *Pushing Up the Sky* (Bruchac & Flavin, 2000). Students enjoyed reading *Knots on a Counting Rope* (Martin, 1997), *The Rough-Face Girl* (Martin, 1998), and *Touching Spirit Bear* (Mikaelsen, 2002).

Mr. Olsen also read aloud engaging texts such as Gregory's (2002) *The Legend of Jimmy Spoon*. This historical fiction novel is based on the true story of Elijah Nicholas Wilson, an 11-year-old who ran away from his pioneer home in Salt Lake City and lived with the Shoshones, led by wise Chief Washakie. Wilson (1919) recounted his own experiences in *White Indian Boy*, also available as *White Indian Boy: My Life Among the Shoshones* (2009). This reading so engaged students that near the end of *The Legend of Jimmy Spoon*, students refused to go to recess, demanding instead that Mr. Olsen keep reading to them.

Students were mesmerized by DeFelice's gripping tale *Weasel* (1991) and eagerly participated in deep discussions and debates regarding the impact of westward expansion on the lives of Native Americans and settlers. Students extended their understanding of these issues as they read about and discussed the Navajo Long Walk, the Cherokee Trail of Tears, and the fate of the Nez Perce.

As a culmination of the unit, students made oral and written presentations for their peers on what they learned. Consistent with a situative theoretical perspective and with the language standards in the CCSS, Mr. Olsen asked students to conduct cooperative research in their small groups. Each group developed a specific oral and then written presentation on Native American tribes from different parts of the country. Their presentations revolved around students' understandings about how the geographic region where the tribe lived influenced their clothing, shelter, diet, beliefs, art, leadership, traditions, legends, and challenges they faced. Students prepared rich presentations that included Internet pictures, illustrations, graphs, charts, and maps, as well as written information that explained the relevant information about their tribes.

Anyone who has conducted units such as these knows that students can learn so much from one another. It is amazing to watch them explain things to one another in ways that adults could not. So, knowledge-building comes about not only from students reading and writing about what they learn, but also through the rich discussions they have with one another.

Throughout the Native American unit, students were taught reading and writing skills and strategies that they employed and demonstrated through their engagement with authentic text, purposeful research and writing, and collaboration with peers while increasing their content knowledge in social studies. Students meaningfully analyzed and discussed varying perspectives of people, characters, authors, and issues that they encountered. Students' motivation and interest extended beyond the classroom. Jessie asked if she could borrow some books and take them home. Due to her enthusiasm about what she was reading about and learning in class, she said her dad wanted to read the books, too. Engaging critical studies like this one are the essence of high-quality instruction that fulfills many of the CCSS standards.

Another Example: Concept-Oriented Reading Instruction

Concept-Oriented Reading Instruction (CORI) is another excellent example of knowledge-building for the purpose of learning about concepts and ideas in the content areas (Guthrie et al., 1999; Guthrie et al., 2000; Swan, 2003). CORI is an instructional framework for motivating students to learn conceptual knowledge. As part of CORI, students engage in direct experiences with a topic to become motivated to study that topic in more depth. The classic example of a CORI activity is the presentation of hermit crabs in the classroom. Students observe real hermit crabs and keep careful records of their observations. Their notes, questions, comments, and observations then become fuel for their researching more about hermit crabs. As they research, they develop reading and study strategies as they search for information. Their research results in meaningful presentations to their peers about what they have learned. The use of CORI meets Anchor Reading Standards 7 and 9 as well as other standards for language and writing. CORI is a rich framework that can guide teachers as they develop lessons and units for knowledge-building. For more information about CORI, see http://www.cori.umd.edu.

SUMMARY

> ➤ A fundamental goal of education is helping students build knowledge about the world.

> ➤ The relationship between background knowledge and reading comprehension is reciprocal—the more one knows about a topic, the better the comprehension of the same topic; the more one reads about a topic, the more one knows.

> ➤ Deep knowledge of a topic better facilitates comprehension than does superficial knowledge. Students with deep knowledge are able to elaborate about a subject. Thus, a fundamental goal of education is to help students build deep knowledge by reading multiple texts and integrating new information with their existing knowledge.

> ➤ Knowledge and strategies are essential. However, a strong knowledge base can make up for a lack of strategies, but strong strategies cannot make up for a lack of knowledge.

Conclusion

The first chapter emphasized the importance of theory and particularly the theoretical frameworks that involved cognitive and situative perspectives in reading. These foundations are helpful in thinking about and planning additional lessons for students to meet all the standards in the CCSS, but especially those that are the focus of this book, Reading Anchor Standards 7 and 9. Throughout this book these perspectives informed the discussions and the many lessons presented.

The cognitive perspective is represented in these few principles to be remembered as teachers ask students to do tasks that meet Standards 7 and 9:

- Students will only learn to the extent to which they can integrate their background knowledge into the new information they are learning.
- Teachers can help students build deep understanding and learning through the use of multiple print texts and online materials.

The situative perspective is represented in these few principles:

- Students can and do learn much from one another as well as from the teacher.
- Teachers can help students build deep understanding and learning through the use of many different support tools, including print texts and online materials.

The truth is that students enjoy and become engaged in learning about the world as we know it. They love learning from the Internet, and they also enjoy learning about challenging ideas. It is the authors' hope that the lessons in the book will help teachers grow in confidence in teaching across multiple texts. While the goal of educators is to meet these challenging new standards, the real joy comes in watching students' enthusiasm for thinking deeply about what they read and see. While the effort may be great, so are the rewards.

Literature References

Adler, D. A. (2005). *A picture book of Frederick Douglass*. New York, NY: Holiday House.

Aguilar, D. A. (2011). *13 planets: The latest view of the solar system*. Washington, DC: National Geographic.

Avi. (2009). *The fighting ground*. New York, NY: HarperCollins.

Bausum, A. (2005). *Freedom riders*. Washington, DC: National Geographic.

Berger, M. (2003). *Spinning spiders*. New York, NY: HarperCollins.

Bishop, N. (2007). *Spiders*. New York, NY: Scholastic.

Brett, J. (1992). *Goldilocks and the three bears*. New York, NY: Putnam.

Brewster, H., & Coulter, L. (1998). *882 ½ Amazing answers to your questions about the Titanic*. New York, NY: Scholastic.

Bruchac, J., & Flavin, T. (2000). *Pushing up the sky: Seven Native American plays for children*. New York, NY: Dial.

Buck, P. S. (1947). *The big wave*. New York, NY: HarperCollins Children's Books.

Buehner, C. (2009). *Goldilocks and the three bears*. London, UK: Puffin.

Carson, M. K. (2012). *Good question: What sank the world's biggest ship and other questions about the Titanic*. New York, NY: Sterling Children's Books.

Clements, A. (1996). *Frindle*. New York, NY: Atheneum Books.

Cline-Ransome, L. C. (2012). *Words set me free: The story of young Frederick Douglass*. New York, NY: Paula Wiseman Books.

Collier, J. L., & Collier, C. (2005). *My brother Sam is dead*. New York, NY: Scholastic.

Cooper, S. (1999). *The dark is rising*. New York, NY: Margaret K. McElderry Books.

Crow, M., Crow, J. M., & Martin, L. R. (1998). *Brave wolf and the thunderbird*. New York, NY: Abbeville Kids.

Cunningham, K. (2011a). *The Navajo*. Danbury, CT: Children's Press.

Cunningham, K. (2011b). *The Sioux*. Danbury, CT: Children's Press.

Cunningham, K. (2011c). *The Wampanoags*. Danbury, CT: Children's Press.

DeFelice, C. (1991). *Weasel*. New York, NY: Avon Camelot.

de Silva, K. (2013). *Bears: Amazing pictures and fun facts on animals in nature*. Seattle, WA: Amazon Digital Services.

DK Publishing. (2007). *Frog: See how they grow*. New York, NY: Author.

Flanagan, A. K. (1998). *The Shawnee*. Danbury, CT: Children's Press.

Freedman, R. (2008). *Freedom walkers: The story of the Montgomery bus boycott*. New York, NY: Holiday House.

George, J. C. (2003). *Julie of the wolves*. New York, NY: Harper Collins.

George, J. C. (2004). *My side of the mountain.* London, UK: Puffin.

Gibbons, G. (1994). *Frogs.* New York, NY: Holiday House.

Goble, P. (1993). *The girl who loved wild horses.* New York, NY: Aladdin.

Goldish, M. (2008). *Beautiful butterflies.* New York, NY: Bearport Publishing.

Graham, I. (2009). *Solar system: A journey to the planets and beyond.* San Diego, CA: Silver Dolphin Books.

Gregory, K. (2002). *The legend of Jimmy Spoon.* New York, NY: HMH Books for Young Readers.

Guernaccia, S. (2010). *Goldilocks and the three bears: A tale moderne.* New York, NY: Harry N. Abrams.

Heiligman, D. (1996). *From caterpillar to butterfly.* New York, NY: HarperCollins.

Henkes, K. (1996). *Lilly's purple plastic purse.* New York, NY: Greenwillow Books.

Hill, R., & Frazier, T. (2010). *Indian nations of North America.* Washington, DC: National Geographic.

Hodge, D., & Stephens, P. (1996). *Bears: Polar bears, black bears and grizzly bears.* Tonawanda, NY: Kids Can Press.

Jenkins, M., & Sanders, B. (2008). *TITANIC disaster at sea.* Somerville, MA: Candlewick Press.

Kajikawa, K. (2009). *Tsunami!* New York, NY: Philomel Books.

Keats, E. J. (1971). *Over in the meadow.* New York, NY: Penguin.

Kennedy, J., & Day, A. (2000). *The teddy bear's picnic.* New York, NY: Aladdin Picture Books.

Korman, G. (2011). *Titanic, book one: Unsinkable.* New York, NY: Scholastic.

Korman, G. (2011). *Titanic, book two: Collision course.* New York, NY: Scholastic.

Korman, G. (2011). *Titanic, book three: S.O.S.* New York, NY: Scholastic.

Lauber, P. (1986). *Volcano: The eruption and healing of Mount St. Helens.* New York, NY: Simon & Schuster.

L'Engle, M. (1962). *A wrinkle in time.* New York, NY: Square Fish.

Levine, E. (1992). *If you traveled West in a covered wagon.* New York, NY: Scholastic.

Levine, E. (1993). *If you traveled on the Underground Railroad.* New York, NY: Scholastic.

Levine, E. (1999). *If you lived with the Iroquois.* New York, NY: Scholastic.

Lewis, C. S. (1994). *The lion, the witch, and the wardrobe.* New York, NY: HarperCollins.

Lobel, A. (2003). *Frog and Toad are friends.* New York, NY: HarperCollins.

Loewen, N., & Avakyan, T. (2011). *Believe me, Goldilocks rocks! The story of the three bears as told by Baby Bear (the other side of the story).* Mankato, MN: Picture Window Books.

Louis, M. (2013). *Monarch butterfly: Caterpillar and butterfly facts for kids.* [Kindle edition]. Available at Amazon.com

Marshall, J. (1998). *Goldilocks and the three bears.* New York, NY: Penguin Group USA.

Marshall, J. (2011). *George and Martha: The best of friends.* New York, NY: Houghton Mifflin Harcourt.

Martin, B. (1996). *Brown bear, brown bear, what do you see?* New York, NY: Henry Holt.

Martin, B. (1997). *Knots on a counting rope.* Los Angeles, CA: Reading Rainbow.

Martin, R. (1998). The *rough-face girl.* London, UK: Puffin.

McDermott, G. (2001). *Raven: A trickster tale from the Pacific Northwest.* New York, NY: HMH Books for Young Readers.

McDonald, J. (2011). *Over in the meadow.* Boston, MA: Barefoot Books.

McGovern, A. (1992). *If you lived with the Sioux.* New York, NY: Scholastic.

McPhail, D. (2005). *The teddy bear.* New York, NY: Squarefish.

McWhorter, D. (2004). *A dream of freedom.* New York, NY: Scholastic.

Messner, K. (2010). *Sugar and ice.* New York, NY: Walker Children's Books.

Micucci, C. (2006). *The life and times of the ant.* New York, NY: Houghton Mifflin Harcourt.

Mikaelsen, B. (2002). *Touching spirit bear.* New York, NY: HarperCollins.

Miller, W. (1996). *Frederick Douglass: The last day of slavery.* New York, NY: Lee & Low.

Moore, K. (1994). *If you lived at the time of the Civil War.* New York, NY: Scholastic.

Moore, K. (1998). *If you lived at the time of the American Revolution.* New York, NY: Scholastic.

Murdoch, D. S. (2005). *DK eyewitness books: North American Indian.* New York, NY: DK Children.

Neye, E. (2000). *Butterflies.* New York, NY: Penguin Young Readers.

O'Dell, S. (1960). *Island of the blue dolphins.* New York, NY: HMH Books for Young Readers.

Oughton, J. (1996). *How the stars fell into the sky.* New York, NY: HMH Books for Young Readers.

Palacio, R. J. (2013). *Wonder.* New York, NY: Knopf.

Paterson, K. (1990). *The tale of the Mandarin ducks.* New York, NY: Scholastic.

Paulsen, G. (1987). *Hatchet.* New York, NY: Simon & Schuster.

Pollock, P. (1996). *The turkey girl: A Zuni story.* New York, NY: Little, Brown & Co.

Roop, P. (1998). *If you lived with the Cherokees.* New York, NY: Scholastic.

Sachar, L. (2000). *Holes.* New York, NY: Dell Yearling Books.

Sendak, M. (1963). *Where the wild things are.* New York, NY: HarperCollins.

Sendak, M. (1970). *In the night kitchen.* New York, NY: HarperCollins.

Sendak, M. (1981). *Outside over there.* New York, NY: HarperCollins.

Scott Foresman. (1990). *Ant cities.* New York, NY: Author.

Shye, M. L. (2013). *Pandas! A kids book about pandas.* Seattle, WA: Amazon Digital Services.

Simon, S. (2006). *Weather.* New York, NY: HarperCollins.

Simon, S. (2007). *Our solar system.* New York, NY: HarperCollins.

Stanley, G. E. (2008). *Frederick Douglass: Abolitionist hero.* New York, NY: Aladdin.

Stead, R. (2009). *When you reach me.* New York, NY: Random House.

Steptoe, J. (1987). *Mufaro's beautiful daughters: An African tale.* Boston, MA: Lothrop.

Stewart, D., & Antram, D. (2013). *You wouldn't want to sail on the Titanic.* New York, NY: Scholastic.

Stewart, M. (2010). *Ants.* Washington, DC: National Geographic.

Stiefel, C. (2009). *Tsunamis* (True Books). Danbury, CT: Childrens Press.

Taylor, T. (2003). *The cay.* New York, NY: Laurel Leaf Publishing.

Time for Kids. (2005). *Time for kids: Bees!* New York, NY: Author.

Uchida, Y. (1984). *Journey to Topaz.* Berkley, CA: Creative Arts Book Company.

Uchida, Y. (1995). *The invisible thread.* Sag Harbor, NY: Beech Tree Books.

Uchida, Y. (1996). *The bracelet.* London, UK: Puffin.

Van Allsburg, C. (1993). *The sweetest fig.* New York, NY: Houghton Mifflin Harcourt.

Wadsworth, O. A. (2002). *Over in the meadow.* New York, NY: North-South Books.

Walsh, K. (2009). *Solar system: A journey to the planets and beyond.* San Diego, CA: Silver Dolphin Books.

Wargin, K. J. (1998). *Legend of sleeping bear.* Ann Arbor, MI: Sleeping Bear Press.

Wiles, D. (2005). *Each little bird that sings.* New York, NY: Houghton Mifflin Harcourt.

Willems, M. (2012). *Goldilocks and the three dinosaurs.* New York, NY: Balzer + Bray.

Wilson, E. N. (1919). *White Indian boy: My life among the Shoshones.* Bel Air, CA: Book Jungle.

Wilson, E. N. (2009). *White Indian boy: My life among the Shoshones.* Colorado Springs, CO: Piccadilly Books.

Wilson, K., & Chapman, J. (2005). *Bear snores on.* New York, NY: Little Simon.

Professional References

Adams, M. J. (1990). *Beginning to read: Thinking and learning about print.* Cambridge, MA: MIT Press.

Adams, M. J. (2010, 2011). Advancing our students' language and literacy: The challenge of complex text. *American Educator, 34*(4), 3–11.

Alexander, P. A. (2002). The development of expertise: The journey from acclimation to proficiency. *Educational Researcher, 32*(8), 10–14.

Alexander, P. A., & Judy, J. E. (1988). The interaction of domain-specific and strategic knowledge in academic performance. *Review of Educational Research, 58*(4), 375–404.

Anderson, J. R., Greeno, J. G., Reder, L., & Simon, H. A. (2000). *Perspectives on learning, thinking, and activity.* Pittsburgh, PA: Carnegie Mellon University, Department of Psychology Paper 3. http://repository.cmu.edu/psychology/3

Anderson, R. C. (1984). Role of the reader's schema in comprehension, learning, and memory. In R. C. Anderson, J. Osborn, & R. J. Tierney (Eds.), *Learning to read in American schools,* (pp. 469–482). Hillsdale, NJ: Erlbaum.

Anderson, R., & Pearson, P. (1984). A schema-theoretic view of basic processes in reading comprehension. In P. D. Pearson, R. Barr, M. L. Kamil, & P. Mosenthal (Eds.), *Handbook of reading research* (pp. 225–253). New York, NY: Longman.

Armbruster, B. B., & Anderson, T. H. (1984). *Producing considerate expository text: Or, easy reading is damned hard writing* (Reading Education Rep. No. 46). Urbana, IL: University of Illinois, Center for the Study of Reading.

Armbruster, B. B., & Nagy, W. E. (1992). Vocabulary in content area lessons. *The Reading Teacher, 45*(7), 550–551.

Atwell, N. (1998). *In the middle.* Portsmouth, NH: Heinemann.

Berliner, D. C. (1986). In pursuit of the expert pedagogue. *Educational Researcher, 15*(7), 5–13.

Bransford, J. D. (1979). *Human cognition: Learning, understanding, and remembering.* Belmont, CA: Wadsworth Publishing.

Brown, J. S., Collins, A., & Duguid, S. (1989). Situated cognition and the culture of learning. *Educational Researcher, 18*(1), 32–42.

Calkins, L. (2010). *Launch an intermediate reading workshop: Getting started with units of study for teaching reading, Grades 3–5.* Portsmouth, NH: Heinemann.

Chall, J. S., & Conrad, S. S. (1991). *Should textbooks challenge students? The case for easier or harder books.* New York, NY: Teachers College Press.

Chase, W. G., & Simon, H. A. (1973). The mind's eye in chess. In W. G. Chase (Ed.), *Visual information processing* (pp. 215–281). New York, NY: Academic Press.

Chi, M. T. H. (1978). Knowledge structures and memory development. In R. S. Sternberg (Ed.), *Children's thinking: What develops?* (pp. 221–229). Hillsdale, NJ: Erlbaum.

Chi, M. T. H., Feltovich, P. J., & Glaser, R. (1981). Categorization and representation of physics problems by experts and novices. *Cognitive Science, 5*(2), 121–152.

Common Core State Standards. (2010). Common Core State Standards Initiative. Available at http://www.corestandards.org

Cott, J. (1983). *Pipers at the gates of dawn: The wisdom of children's literature*. New York, NY: Random House.

Dole, J. A., Nokes, J. D., & Drits, D. (2010). Cognitive strategy instruction. In G. G. Duffy & S. E. Israel (Eds.), *Handbook of research on reading comprehension* (pp. 347–372). New York, NY: Routledge.

Duke, N. K. (2000). 3.6 minutes per day: The scarcity of informational text in first grade. *Reading Research Quarterly, 35*(2), 202–224.

Fitzgerald, J. (1989). Research on stories: Implications for teachers. In K. D. Muth (Ed.), *Children's comprehension of text: Research into practice* (pp. 2–36). Newark, DE: International Reading Association.

Gillespie, J. (2005). "It would be fun to do again": Multigenre responses to literature. *Journal of Adolescent and Adult Literacy, 48*(8), 678–684.

Goldman, S. R. (2004). Cognitive aspects of constructing meaning through and across texts. In N. W. Shuart-Ferris & D. Bloome (Eds.), *Intertextuality and research on classroom education* (pp. 313–347). Greenwich, CT: Information Age Publishing.

Goldman, S. R., Meyerson, P., Wolfe, M., Mayfield, C., Coté, N., & Bloom, D. (1999, April). *"If it says so in the text book, it must be true": Multiple sources in the middle school social studies classroom.* Paper presented at the symposium "Multiple Text, Multiple Source Theories of Reading and Learning in Social Studies" of the American Educational Research Association, Montreal, Canada.

Graesser, A. C., Golding, J. M., & Long, D. L. (1991). Narrative representations and comprehension. In R. Barr, M. L. Kamil, P. Mosenthal, & P. D. Pearson (Eds.), *Handbook of reading research* (Vol. 2, pp. 171–205). New York, NY: Longman.

Guthrie, J. T., Anderson, E., Alao, S., & Rinehart, J. (1999). Influences of concept-oriented reading instruction on strategy use and conceptual learning from text. *Elementary School Journal, 99*(4), 343–366.

Guthrie, J. T., Cox, K. E., Knowles, K. T., Buehl, M., Mazzoni, S. A., & Fasulo, L. (2000). In L. Baker, J. T. Guthrie, & M. J. Dreher (Eds.), *Engaging young readers: Promoting achievement and motivation,* (pp. 209–236). New York, NY: Guilford.

Hartman, D. (1995). Eight readers reading: The intertextual links of proficient readers reading multiple passages. *Reading Research Quarterly, 30*(3), 520–560.

Hartman, D. K., & Hartman, J. A. (1993). Reading across texts: Expanding the role of the reader. *The Reading Teacher, 47*(3), 202–211.

Harvey, S., & Goudvis, A. (2007). *Strategies that work: Teaching comprehension for understanding and engagement*. Boston, MA: Stenhouse.

Hiebert, E. H. (2010). *Unique words require unique instruction: Teaching words in stories and informational books*. Santa Cruz, CA: TextProject. Available at http://www.textproject.org/professional-development/text-matters/unique-words-require-unique-instruction

Hiebert, E. H. (2011). Growing capacity with literary vocabulary: The megaclusters framework. *American Reading Forum Annual Yearbook* [Online], Vol. 31. http://americanreadingforum.org/yearbook/11_yearbook/documents/Hiebert%20KEYNOTE.pdf

Hiebert, E. H. (2012). Core vocabulary: The foundation for successful reading of complex text. *Text Matters* 1.2. Santa Cruz, CA: TextProject. Available at http://textproject.org/professional-development/text-matters/core-vocabulary/

Hiebert, E. H. (2013). Core vocabulary and the challenge of complex text. In S. Neuman & L. Gambrell (Eds.), *Reading research in the age of the Common Core State Standards*. Newark, DE: International Reading Association.

Johnson-Laird, P. N. (1989). Mental models. In M. I. Posner (Ed.), *Foundations of cognitive science* (pp. 469–499). Cambridge, MA: MIT Press.

Kamil, M. L., Borman, G. D., Dole, J., Kral, C. C., Salinger, T., Torgesen, J., Cai, X., Helsel, F., Yael, K., & Spier, E. (2008). *Improving adolescent literacy: Effective classroom and intervention practices: A practice guide*. Washington, DC: National Center for Education Evaluation and Regional Assistance, Institute of Education Sciences, U.S. Department of Education.

Kintsch, W. (2004). The construction-integration model of text comprehension and its implications for instruction. In R. B. Ruddell & N. J. Unrau (Eds.), *Theoretical models and processes of reading* (pp. 1270–1380). Newark, DE: International Reading Association.

Klingner, J. K., & Vaughn, S. (1998). Using collaborative strategic reading. *Teaching Exceptional Children, 30*(6), 32–37.

Klingner, J. K., Vaughn, S., & Schumm, J. S. (1998). Collaborative strategic reading during social studies in heterogeneous fourth-grade classrooms. *The Elementary School Journal, 99*(1), 3–22.

Krathwohl, D. R. (2002). A revision of Bloom's Taxonomy: An overview. *Theory into Practice, 41*(4), 212–225.

Mandler, J. M., & Johnson, N. S. (1977). Remembrance of things parsed: Story structure and recall. *Cognitive Psychology, 9*(1), 111–151.

McConaughy, S. H. (1982). Developmental changes in story comprehension and levels of questioning. *Language Arts, 59*(6), 580–589, 600.

McKeown, M. G., Beck, I. L., & Blake, R. G. K. (2009). Rethinking reading comprehension instruction: A comparison of instruction for strategies and content approaches. *Reading Research Quarterly, 44*(3), 218–253.

Menke, D. J., & Pressley, M. (1994). Elaborative interrogation: Using "Why" questions to enhance the learning from text. *Journal of Reading, 37*(8), 642–645.

Meyer, B. J. F. (1975). *The organization of prose and its effects on memory.* Amsterdam, The Netherlands: North-Holland.

Mohr, K. A. J. (2003). Children's choices: A comparison of book preferences between Hispanic and non-Hispanic first graders. *Reading Psychology: An International Quarterly, 24*(2), 163–176.

Murphy, P. K., & Alexander, P. A. (2002). What counts? The predictive power of subject-matter knowledge, strategic processing, and interest in domain-specific performance. *Journal of Experimental Education, 70*(3), 197–214.

National Assessment Governing Board. (2011). *Reading framework for the 2011 National Assessment of Educational Progress.* Washington, DC: Author.

National Assessment Governing Board. (2013). *Reading framework for the 2013 National Assessment of Educational Progress.* Washington, DC: Author.

National Institute of Child Health and Human Development. (2000). *Report of the National Reading Panel. Teaching children to read: An evidence-based assessment of the scientific research literature on reading and its implications for reading instruction* (NIH Publication).

Neuman, S. (2006). How we neglect knowledge and why. *American Educator, 30*(1), 24–27.

Recht, D. R., & Leslie, L. (1988). Effect of prior knowledge on good and poor readers' memory of text. *Journal of Educational Psychology, 80*(1), 16–20.

Romano, T. (2000). *Writing multigenre papers.* Portsmouth, NH: Heinemann.

Shanahan, T., Callison, K., Carriere, C., Duke, N. K., Pearson, P. D., Schnatschneider, C., & Torgesen, J. (2010). *Improving reading comprehension in kindergarten through 3rd grade: A practice guide* (NCEE 2010-4038). Washington, DC: National Center for Education and Evaluation and Regional Assistance, Institute of Education Sciences, U.S. Department of Education.

Singer, H., & Donlan, D. (1982). Active comprehension: Problem-solving schema with question generation for comprehension of complex short stories. *Reading Research Quarterly, 17*(2), 166–185.

Smith, N. B. (1965). *American reading instruction.* Newark, DE: International Reading Association.

Spilich, G. J., Vesonder, G. T., Chiesi, H. L., & Voss, J. F. (1979). Text processing of domain-related information for individuals with high and low domain knowledge. *Journal of Verbal Learning and Verbal Behavior, 18*, 275–290.

Stein, N., & Glenn, C. G. (1979). An analysis of story comprehension in elementary school children. In R. Freedle (Ed.), *Discourse production and comprehension* (Vol. 1, pp. 53–119). Norwood, NJ: Ablex.

Swan, E. A. (2003). *Concept-oriented reading instruction: Engaging classrooms, lifelong learners.* New York, NY: Guilford Press.

VanSledright, B. A., & Kelly, C. (1998). Reading American history: The influence of using multiple sources on six fifth graders. *The Elementary School Journal, 98*(3), 239–265.

Vaughn, S., Klingner, J. K., & Bryant, D. P. (2001). Collaborative Strategic Reading as a means to enhance peer-mediated instruction for reading comprehension and content-area learning. *Remedial and Special Education, 22*(2), 66–74.

Walsh, K. (2013). *The solar system.* Time for kids nonfiction readers, 2nd edition. Huntington Beach, CA: Teacher Created Materials.

Webb, N. L. (2002). *Depth of knowledge questions for four content areas.* Available at http://ossucurr.pbworks.com/w/file/fetch/49691156/Norm%20web%20dok%20by%20subject%20area.pdf

Willingham, D. T. (2006). *Cognition: The thinking animal.* New York, NY: Pearson.

Wolfersberger, M. E., Reutzel, D. R., Sudweeks, R., & Fawson, P. C. (2004). Developing and validating the Classroom Literacy Environmental Profile (CLEP): A tool for examining the "print richness" of early childhood and elementary classrooms. *Journal of Literacy Research, 36*(2), 211–272.

Woloshyn, V. E., Pressley, M., & Schneider, W. (1992). Elaborative-interrogation and prior-knowledge effects on learning of facts. *Journal of Educational Psychology, 84*(1), 115–124.

Index

About the Authors

Janice A. Dole is professor of education and director of the reading and literacy program in the Department of Educational Psychology at the University of Utah. She has taught elementary and middle school students in Massachusetts, California, and Colorado. Her areas of research include comprehension instruction, school reform, and professional development. She has published widely in the areas of comprehension instruction and more recently in professional development and school reform. Her publications include articles in *Reading Research Quarterly*, *Review of Educational Research*, *The Elementary School Journal*, and *The Reading Teacher*. She has been a contributing consultant for over 30 years to the National Assessment of Educational Progress. She frequently consults on a national level, traveling around the country as well as internationally, speaking to teachers, literacy coaches, and administrators on reading issues.

Brady E. Donaldson is currently a literacy coach for the Salt Lake City School District. He earned his master's degree and Ph.D. at Utah State University. Brady's career includes over 20 years teaching at both the primary- and intermediate-grade levels in Title I and non–Title I schools. He has extensive experience working directly with students, classroom teachers, and literacy coaches. After leaving the classroom, he focused his efforts on coordinating and developing professional development for classroom teachers in the areas of reading and writing instruction. He worked as the district director of Reading First in a local Utah district from 2006–2009. His work in Reading First required him to oversee the work of several literacy coaches as well as the budget and overall coordination of Reading First in the district. In addition, he regularly teaches graduate courses in reading and literacy for the Utah reading endorsement at local universities. His current interests and areas of expertise include foundational skills in reading as well as comprehension development and instruction.

Rebecca S. Donaldson completed her master's and Ph.D. at Utah State University. She currently serves as Title I Instructional Improvement Specialist for the Utah State Office of Education. She has been an enthusiastic educator for over 30 years. Literacy instruction has been her professional passion throughout her career. In addition to spending 17 years as a classroom teacher in grades 1–5, she has also enjoyed working as a reading specialist, literacy coach, professional developer, and adjunct professor at local universities. Becky served as the Utah Reading First Director from 2002–2010 and was the 2011–2012 President of the Utah Council of the International Reading Association. In 2013, she was a Distinguished Finalist for the International Reading Association Outstanding Dissertation of the Year Award.